ANGELS OF MERCY . . .

Here are the stories of . . . Joy Snell, an English nurse who was assisted in her hospital work by three angels, and who actually witnessed a "take-away" angel at the deathbed of a seventeen-year-old girl . . . Patricia P., who was frantically trying to reach her two-year-old niece in a swimming pool when she heard an angel's voice say calmly, "Swim to her," enabling her to save the little girl from drowning . . . Jane M. Howard, whose guardian angel directed her to buy a pair of angel-shaped earrings. One month later, she had a phone call from a friend who'd just been diagnosed with cancer, and after the call, Jane was encircled by angels who told her to go home and wrap the earrings for her friend, with a special message of love and healing from the angels. . . .

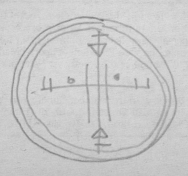

Books by Rosemary Ellen Guiley

Angels of Mercy
Tales of Reincarnation
Vampires Among Us

Published by POCKET BOOKS

Angels of
Mercy

Rosemary Ellen
Guiley

POCKET BOOKS

New York   London   Toronto   Sydney   Tokyo   Singapore

An *Original* Publication of POCKET BOOKS

POCKET BOOKS, a division of Simon & Schuster Inc.
1230 Avenue of the Americas, New York, NY 10020

Copyright © 1994 by Rosemary Ellen Guiley

All rights reserved, including the right to reproduce
this book or portions thereof in any form whatsoever.
For information address Pocket Books, 1230 Avenue
of the Americas, New York, NY 10020

ISBN: 0-671-77094-2

First Pocket Books printing April 1994

10 9 8 7 6 5 4 3 2 1

POCKET and colophon are registered trademarks of
Simon & Schuster Inc.

Cover photo courtesy of Scala/Art Resource, N.Y.

Printed in the U.S.A.

For Sue Robinson
Alis volat propriis

Acknowledgments

I would like to thank all the people who granted me interviews for this book, for their generous sharing of personal experiences. I also would like to thank all the people who wrote to me to tell me about their experiences. I received more stories than I was able to use, and I am sorry that I could not accommodate them all. The angels are busy.

In addition, I'm deeply appreciative to Doreen M. Beauregard for her help in the material concerning the history of beliefs about angels, the images of angels, and guardian angels.

My thanks again to Claire Zion, associate executive editor at Pocket Books, for enabling this book to come into being.

Contents

Introduction

For many years, I have felt the presence of guiding beings in my life. I cannot pinpoint when my awareness opened to them; rather, it seemed to be a gradual expansion of consciousness that reached out beyond the physical realm, the way the rays of the dawning sun gradually penetrate the darkness of the night. The presence of these beings became more pronounced in adulthood after I embarked in earnest on my own spiritual quest, both personally and professionally. The more I focused my attention on them, the more defined these beings became.

My initial intuitive sense was that these helping beings were "angels," and that is what I have always called them. The interpretation of nonphysical entities is subjective—what one person calls an angel, another will call, for example, the guiding presence of Jesus, or the Virgin Mary, or God, or Goddess, or the spirit of a beloved one who has died, or an animal spirit guide. As you will see in this book, impressions of angels are subjective and vary considerably.

My strongest sense of the presence of angels concerns my work as a writer. Rare is the artist who does not acknowledge being inspired and influenced by something greater than the self. I feel that angels facilitate my work in numerous ways. They are conduits of the inspiration and creative energy that enable the assembly of information and words into something meaningful. They orchestrate all the marvelous synchronicities that lead me to the opportunities, people, and resources I need to execute my work. They provide guidance in the form of ideas, either my own or presented by others. They communicate through the promptings of the inner voice, intuition, dreams, and, occasionally, through dramatic appearances in the physical plane.

I am often asked if I think my writing is a channeling of angels. I do not. I do not go into trance, nor do I do automatic writing. I believe I create on my own, and I am fully present during the process. But I also believe I am assisted and influenced by angels. I am grateful for their help, and I acknowledge them daily in my meditation.

I sense a small group of angels who are around me all the time, connected to my personal and professional lives. They are joined by other angels who come and go depending on circumstances. Perhaps angels, in their individual expressions, have "specialties" such as humans have in order to make a living. New book or article projects invariably bring me an influx of angelic visitors, who take up the front lines while other angels then fade into the background. Such visitors remain until their presence is superseded by other angels for other purposes.

When I began work on *Angels of Mercy,* the angels came out in force. It seemed I had a small army looking over my shoulder to weigh in with their various influences. When I set off to interview someone, my angelic band came with me and was joined by another band of angels attached to the person I was meeting. Indeed, David Cousins, a clairvoyant and healer whom I met at his home in Cardiff, Wales, commented that the room was packed with angels who wished to participate in our conversation.

When I fell behind schedule in my work on the book, the angels intervened with an unusually loud voice. Normally they don't ride me about my deadlines. But turmoil in my personal life threw my work into a tailspin for months, and the angels seemed anxious that "their" book not suffer. The inner voice reminded me emphatically not to neglect the book, to get it done as soon as possible. Intervention also came on the physical plane. People with whom I had not spoken in months, and who in the past had evinced little interest in the nuts and bolts of my work, called me to inquire about progress on the angel book and to urge me to finish it so that it could be published soon.

Alas, even the angels could not keep me on schedule, and I had to get a significant extension of my deadline. But angels keep the faith even when we stumble, and they are patient. They waited for me to get my personal life back on an even keel, and when I resumed work on the book, they chimed back in with as much enthusiasm as ever.

In addition to my writing, I lecture a great deal, and

I feel the guiding presence of a "speaking angel." I have never seen him—though others have—but I sense his presence. He is a facilitator who helps me organize and deliver talks.

Angels do much more than guide us in our work. There are angels that look after our relationships, our health, our spiritual growth, and our homes. There are angels that come into our lives just to assist us with major transitions. There are angels that accompany us when we travel. Whenever I drive in my car, I visualize "traveling angels" riding on the hood, trunk, and roof and clinging to the sides. Whenever I fly in a plane, there is always a band of angels flying along with the craft.

Sometimes angels arrive in our lives with a single-purpose mission and depart when that mission is accomplished. When I was going through a lot of personal turmoil, which involved the breakup of my marriage, an upheaval in my work, and more than one relocation, I was assisted by angels of healing. During the rough passage, I went to England to conduct research for this and other books. I visited my dear friend Eddie Burks, a wonderful clairvoyant and healer whose remarkable experiences are related in chapter 8. In fact, it was *Angels of Mercy* that had led to our meeting the previous year, and we had become fast friends. (Undoubtedly, the angels had brought us together for more than one purpose!) On my last day in England, Eddie gave me a healing, for I was in a raw state. As he drove me to Heathrow airport to catch my flight for the States, he sensed a presence come into my aura. This being, or angel as I would call it, had arrived for the sole purpose of flying home with me, to wrap me in a loving blanket of energy that would help heal me and restore my vitality during the flight. Indeed, I felt more calm and relaxed during the flight than I had for weeks. A skeptic would call this the result of the power of suggestion, but I prefer to think of it as the loving touch of an angel. It was by no means a wonder cure. I still had a long and bumpy emotional road ahead of me, but the angel helped me to recharge at a time when I seemed precariously low on emotional resources.

I believe in angels, and I believe that the more we believe in angels, the more they manifest in our lives. That has certainly been my own experience, and the people who shared their experiences for this book attest to that as well. Angels are ready to help us. All we have to do is acknowledge them.

Rosemary Ellen Guiley
Baltimore, 1993

Angels of Mercy

1

Enter Angels

Robert S., an industrial electrician who lives near Trenton, New Jersey, owes his life to an angel. While working in a mill, he grabbed hold of a killer 440-volt wire that he didn't know was live. As he felt the electricity surge through his body, he thought, "My God, I don't want to die!"

Instantly, he was pulled off the wire by an invisible pair of hands around his waist. He was hurled violently backward and fell to the floor. The next thing he knew, he was lying on his back, looking up at a coworker. He should have been dead.

Robert's coworkers said that his life had been saved by the fact that he was wearing new shoes that day, and the thick rubber soles afforded insulation. Robert believes differently. "I felt something pull me off," he said. "Something saved my life. I thank God I'm alive." That "something," he thinks, was his guardian angel.

Robert suffered some third-degree burns and lost a little finger to gangrene. Within two years of the accident he developed psoriasis. Irritated patches of skin appeared around his waist. One day he noticed that the patches matched where he had felt the invisible hands grab him that fateful day. The association was eerie, and it reinforced his conviction that divine intervention on the part of one of God's messengers had rescued him from death. The experience had a profound impact on him. Like most people who have what researchers call an "extraordinary experience" or "exceptional experience" involving elements of the unknown, Robert had difficulty talking about it to others. When he related the story to me, he hadn't mentioned it to anyone for years.

Not far from Robert is Alice Haggerty, who lives in Trenton. Alice feels she, too, was saved from the brink of death by her guardian angel. Her experience is much different from Robert's, but both are testimony to the dramatic yet versatile ways that angels intervene in our lives.

"When I was seven years old, I got sick with diphtheria," Alice told me. "I was sick for about ten days. My family was living in a Mennonite community in Philadelphia—I was raised Mennonite. We had very strong beliefs about God, the Bible, and angels. We did not believe in hospitals or extra medicine—doctors, yes. While I was sick, a doctor came to the house about every day. Medicine was not helping. He wanted to hospitalize me, but it was against our religion.

"I was in and out of delirium from the high fever. But I overheard him one day tell my parents out in the hall that I wasn't going to make it through the night.

Strangely, I didn't have any fear about it. I looked forward to going to heaven.

"That night there was a thunderstorm outside. My parents eventually got tired and went to bed. While I was asleep, an angel came into the room. I thought I had died and the angel was going to take me to heaven. He was bigger than a person, and had long hair and flowing robes, and was glowing. I never saw a face. He communicated through my thoughts that he was going to make me better.

"The angel put a silver belt around my waist, picked me up and cradled me in his arms, and took me out the second-floor window, which was closed and had a screen. I could feel a tingling sensation in my body as we went through the window. We went out over a tree. I could see light in the distance. I thought it was the entrance to heaven. We went toward it and entered the light, but I don't know what happened there.

"The next thing I knew, the angel was laying me back down in bed. It was morning, and I woke up. I was soaking wet and the bedsheets were wet. And I was one hundred percent better.

"I jumped out of bed and went running into my parents' room shouting, 'Mom, I'm starving!' She was astonished to see me and ordered me back to bed. The doctor was summoned. He came and examined me and couldn't understand how the diphtheria had disappeared. It was a miracle."

After her recovery, Alice started to draw angels, and had an increased interest in the Bible.

"Being with this angel was wonderful," she recalled. "It was the most peaceful, loving feeling I've ever had in my life. Just to have that experience again would be a dream."

Alice tried to tell her mother about the angel, but she rejected the story and warned Alice that she was dabbling with evil spirits. She even took Alice to see their pastor about the possibility, and put a hex sign on the front door to ward off evil influences. It was not until many years later that she accepted Alice's explanation of what happened that night.

I wondered if the silver belt used by the angel had been the silvery cord that connects the astral body to the physical body. The silvery cord is sometimes seen by persons who have out-of-body experiences. It remains intact until death, when the soul is freed from the body. Alice agreed with this interpretation—that her astral cord had been secured about her by the angel.

She had a second experience when her guardian angel appeared to her. "I was thirteen, and we had just moved to a new house in Philadelphia. I was sleeping in bed, in a room with my two sisters. I shared a double bed with my younger sister. I was against a wall. One night something made me jump awake. My sisters stayed asleep. The room had a strange, bright glow. I looked up and there was the angel hovering near the ceiling. I was looking at it, seeing the same long hair and flowing robes. The next thing I knew, I was up there with the angel, looking down at my body in bed. Somehow, this didn't seem unusual to me. I felt the strange tingling again. It seemed like it was quite a while that I was with the angel, and we were communicating, but I don't know about what. We may have even gone somewhere. Then the next thing I knew, I was jumping back in my body. I looked up, thinking, 'Don't go away!' I felt the same awe and sense of beauty and loving feeling that I'd had when

4

the angel healed me, and I felt a tremendous longing to be with the angel."

This time, Alice decided not to talk about it, to avoid ridicule and denial. "After that, I would sometimes lay awake at night wishing for the angel to come back," she said. "But I've never seen an angel again. I've been out of my body many times since then, however, and I feel I am accompanied by an invisible presence, probably my angel. It envelops me. I do feel it has a personality. It's very hard to put into words."

For Aimeé S. Lacombe of Cambria, California, her angelic rescuer appeared in the form of a human being. Here is her account:

"I was in a hospital suffering from some rare throat virus that caused me to cough so violently, I would begin to strangle. During one of those fits in the middle of the night, I called for a nurse. No one came right away, and I began to panic, for I couldn't breathe.

"Suddenly the door flew open and a short, stocky nurse came bursting in, and with a voice of authority said, 'Close your mouth and breathe through your nose.' When I gestured that no air would come through my nose, she clamped her hand over my mouth and shouted, 'Breathe!' And breathe I did, and I stopped choking. Her next words were, 'Just can't understand why they haven't taught you that.' And out she went.

"Because I wanted to thank her, the next morning I asked the nurse who it was who was on night duty. When she asked me to describe her, she looked puzzled and said that description didn't fit anyone on their staff, but she would check on it.

"Later, the head nurse came in and asked me to

describe the nurse again. She said there was no one employed there who came close to my description. When I asked why they hadn't instructed me on what to do when I began to strangle, they said they had never heard of the method.

"The doctor's response to the experience was interesting. He knew about the method, but why he hadn't told me, I'll never know. But he whispered in my ear, 'I think you met an angel.' By then, I was convinced I had.

"There have been a few times in my life when an almost overpowering aroma of flowers would occur, when no flowers were near. With it was always a sensation of euphoria. I do not think that I am anyone 'special' because of these experiences. But, through them and other spiritual happenings, I know we are here to evolve back to the spirit that we truly are. And once we believe we are not victims of life but the creators of our reality, all manner of beautiful manifestations appear in our life."

Robert, Alice, and Aimeé have plenty of company. In recent years, angels have made a tremendous comeback and have undergone a resurgence of popularity. More than at any other time in modern history, people are believing in angels and are talking about their encounters with them. Books on angels proliferate. Not only are people interested in angels, they want to learn how to communicate with God's emissaries. In the United States, angel workshops and seminars draw large crowds. The first international "Be An Angel Day" took place on August 22, 1993. Organized by Jane M. Howard, a Maryland channeler of angels and author and lecturer, the campaign urged people to be angels by doing an act of service for someone on that day.

It wasn't long ago that angels gathered dust, consigned to art and Christmas cards. Except for Catholicism's cult of the guardian angel, most Westerners have scoffed at the idea that angels might be real. Even in the early 1980s, Dutch physician H. C. Moolenburgh found that people laughed at him when he asked if they believed in angels or had ever encountered an angel. A few people who admitted having encounters with angels were afraid to talk about them, out of fear that others would think they were crazy. Undaunted, Moolenburgh wrote *A Handbook of Angels*. A few years later, the book became an international hit.

Similarly, French journalist Georges Huber encountered a great deal of skepticism about angels when he began research for his book, *My Angel Will Go Before You,* published in 1983. Huber virtually apologizes for his interest in angels, in an age in which science and technology make them seem hopelessly out of date and the stuff of fairy tales. A letter preface to his book from Sighard Kleiner, abbot general of the Cistercians, comments, "I was very surprised to learn recently that you were going to bring out a book on angels. A journalist, even though he is well versed in theology: isn't that a rather daring subject for him to choose? Don't journalists always go where the wind blows? You could scarcely say the wind is blowing around angels these days."

Indeed, the ecclesiastical world has been almost embarrassed over the question of the existence of angels. Church figures from various denominations have suggested that the concept of angels is "out of touch with reality" and thus endangers our belief in the Gospels, and that it would be best for all if angels simply disappeared from the liturgy, from sermons—and from public awareness.

Writing in 1969, Cardinal G. M. Garrone, the archbishop of Toulouse, asserted that "it is an understatement to say that angels have gone out of style. We prefer not to think of them for fear of being confronted with a painful and insoluble dilemma. Either we must affirm with the Church the existence of these mysterious beings and thus find ourselves in the disagreeable company of the naive and uninformed, or else frankly speak out against their existence and be in the equally unpleasant situation of rejecting the faith of the Church and the obvious meaning of the Gospels. The majority, therefore, choose to express no opinion at all."

Angels, however, refuse to be consigned to a liturgical wastebasket. Popular belief in them will not go away. In fact, belief in angels is at an all-time high, rivaling the level of belief that peaked during the Middle Ages. More than ever, we *need* angels.

What accounts for this new popularity of angels? There are several major factors. Perhaps the leading factor is a collective sense of lack of control. Every day we turn on the radio or television and get a litany of bad news. We feel overwhelmed by pressures and circumstances that seem beyond our influence: drugs, crime, homelessness, economic problems, political and social instability, war, disease, famine, and an increasingly toxic environment. We long for help—some sort of divine intervention that, if it cannot change things on a large scale, can at least brighten our own circumstances.

Another significant factor in the popularity of angels is that they are an appealing form of divine intervention. Unlike the Judeo-Christian God, who is abstract and has no form or face, angels are personable. According to our mythology, they can assume the form of beautiful humans. They are loving, benevolent, wise, patient, and capable of bestowing miracles—or so we perceive them (according to Scripture, however, angels will punish humans if that is God's directive). We view angels as always with us—they never desert us, no matter how poorly we perform. And even though they do not always save us from catastrophe, they stand ready as a source of strength to help us through all our trials. We seem to have a great, collective hunger for spiritual guidance that is personal and intimate, a hunger that is not being met through conventional religion. Angels are our personal companions, our guides, our protectors.

Another major factor in their current popularity is our increasing openness to paranormal experience. Popular interest in the paranormal and things spiritual has gone through cycles in the past. The present interest is part of the so-called Aquarian Age or New Age, which gained momentum around the 1960s. In the 1980s, actress Shirley MacLaine encouraged candor and exploration with publication of her own spiritual quests.

Michael's Request

A most unusual angel encounter, which involved the archangel Michael, happened to a dear friend of mine, Juliet Hollister, of Greenwich, Connecticut. The encounter is unusual because it featured a vivid visual apparition, clear telepathic communication, some odd synchronicities with other people, and a demonstration that even angels like to have a good time.

Juliet is founder of the Temple of Understanding, the second-oldest interfaith organization in the world. Its purpose is to be a "spiritual United Nations," promoting understanding among and about the world's religions. Juliet conceived of the idea for the temple in 1959, and launched it with the help of Eleanor Roosevelt. To build the temple, Juliet has traveled the world and has had audiences with and been entertained by an impressive list of heads of state, spiritual leaders, and other luminaries. She has met three popes—Paul II, John XXIII, and John Paul I—as well as the Dalai Lama, with whom she corresponds regularly. She has traveled to some of the remotest and wildest corners of the earth. Juliet has packed more adventures and accomplishments into the second half of her life than most people could manage in several lifetimes. Some of her friends call her a "spiritual Auntie Mame," a moniker that suits her well—she is charming, sophisticated, funny, and irreverent, and always ready to set off on yet another adventure.

One might think that Juliet's work with the leaders of the world's major religions would bring her into constant contact with the angel kingdom. Far from it. Many of the leaders with whom she works are openly skeptical of the existence of angels, considering them metaphors or literary devices. Consequently, for the first twenty-five years that she was developing the

Temple of Understanding, Juliet kept quiet about her own beliefs and experiences.

Her earliest encounter with other worlds took place when she was a child growing up in a suburb of New York. Her mother was a Christian Scientist and former Baltimore debutante. Juliet was fond of her grandfather (on her mother's side) and looked forward every summer to visits at his home, Bunker Hill Farms, outside of Baltimore. One afternoon in 1920, when Juliet was eight, her mother told her, "Grandpa has gone to another world." Two years later, when Juliet once again visited Bunker Hill Farms, she looked up from playing in the garden to see Grandpa, looking solid and real, as if he were still alive. She received a mental message: "Surprised, aren't you, little granddaughter? I just popped by to let you know I am keeping an eye on you." And with that, he was gone.

Juliet told her mother, who dismissed the episode as a trick of afternoon sunlight and a child's imagination. Juliet knew better and repressed talking about Grandpa's visit. It marked her first spiritual turning point, for it sparked a curiosity to investigate other religions.

"I have always believed in angels," Juliet told me one snowy winter morning as we sat in her cozy Greenwich cottage furnished with items collected on her round-the-world adventures. Like her experience with her grandfather, she had kept these beliefs private, lest others disapprove.

One of her first angel events was a vicarious experience through her young son, Dickerman, who is now a prominent doctor in the cancer field. Dickie, as Juliet called him when he was small, became interested in angels when he was about five or six years old—the most common age for an initial "extraordinary experience," according to research.

One day Dickie announced to Juliet, "More than anything in the world, I want to see an angel. Can you do something to help, Mom?"

Juliet thought for a moment. "Every night after I tuck you into bed and you say your prayers, why don't you quietly ask an angel to come and see you?" She wasn't at all sure that this request would work, but she felt she had to say something.

Dickie thought it was a good idea. So, every night he asked for an angel to come. But nothing happened. About once a week he would say to Juliet, "No angel, but I'm keeping asking, Mom." He seemed so earnest and patient.

After awhile, Juliet began to get a little cross with the angelic kingdom for not responding. Finally one day Dickie burst into his parents' bedroom at six in the morning, bounced on the bed, and announced, "The angel came, Mom!" He was *so* excited.

Juliet was thrilled. "Tell me all about it," she urged.

"He was huge, standing in the corner of my bedroom," said Dickie. "I felt all this wonderful warm loving thing, and I knew it was an angel."

"What did he look like? Was it a boy or a girl?"

"I really don't know," answered Dickie, "because the angel told me that he was afraid that if I looked into his face, it would be so full of light that I would be frightened. So he purposely kept his back to me."

That was Dickie's only visit by an angel—at least that he ever talked about.

Juliet's encounter with the archangel Michael took place in October 1984, as she was preparing for the sixth Spirit Summit Conference sponsored by the Temple of Understanding. The first conference had been held in India in 1968, and others had followed at intervals of several years in Geneva and in the United States. This sixth conference was to take place at St. John the Divine, the largest Gothic cathedral in the world, located on the Upper West Side in Manhattan. Numerous luminaries of the ecclesiastical and political worlds were featured guests, including His Holiness the Dalai Lama, Tenzin Gyatso, and Dr. Robert Mueller, assistant secretary-general of the United Nations. The audience was expected to number eight to ten thousand people—a standing-room-only crowd inside the giant and elegant cathedral.

At the end of the daylong conference, a candlelight ceremony was scheduled to take place. Various religious leaders would carry candles to the center altar and say prayers from their respective religions. Juliet was to be included in this ceremony, delivering a fifteen-minute talk on the temple, its purpose, and its activities.

The prospect of making a speech in front of so many of the world's religious leaders and so many people made Juliet nervous. She slaved away over her speech and rehearsed it again and again.

The conference was on Saturday, October 7. The final rehearsal was slated for the Friday night before. Juliet traveled from Connecticut to Manhattan on Friday afternoon and settled into a room at the Cosmopolitan Club, located at Sixty-sixth Street and Park Avenue on the East Side. She took a shower and lay down to rest.

As she was getting ready to rise and dress, Juliet suddenly became aware of a presence, in the form of a huge column of light, standing at the foot of her bed. She perceived the outline of a figure and sensed that it was an angel, though she did not see wings or a face.

Juliet was startled but not frightened. She'd believed in angels all of her life, and knew they didn't show up without good reason—just to check out a hairdo, as she put it later. As she studied it, the presence began to communicate telepathically with her.

"You're going to be speaking at the cathedral, and angels have a lot to do with holy, sacred places," the angel told her. "We guard them. Millions of people don't believe in us, but we are real entities. On behalf of the angelic kingdom, we would appreciate it if, when you make your speech, you would tell the people about us, that we are real, that we love the human race, and that we would like to work on behalf of it. But we can't unless we're invited to do so. We don't enter the life of a human unless we're asked. We are very eager to help."

This message overwhelmed Juliet. Never had she thought of saying anything about angels in her little speech. She replied to the figure of light, "I really do believe you're an angel. In fact, I kind of think you're the archangel Michael, although there's no reason why I should have one of the top ones show up. I'd love to do anything to help this planet and all the people on it, but I don't altogether trust myself here. I tell you what, I'll make a bargain with you. I'll do it if you do something to confirm that I'm not hallucinating, that I've got this straight."

The form of light disappeared. Juliet rose, dressed, and walked down to the corner of Sixty-sixth Street and Park Avenue to hail a taxi to go to the cathedral. It was a blowing, cold evening at rush hour on a Friday night. Anyone who has ever been in New York City under those conditions knows how difficult it is to find a free taxi. Dozens and dozens roar by, all occupied, no matter where you are in that huge city. Juliet stood on the corner waiting in vain for a cab. Fifteen, twenty minutes went by. She grew anxious about arriving on time for the rehearsal.

Then she was struck by what seemed to be a brilliant idea. (In retrospect, she believed the idea was planted by the angelic form that had visited her in the room. "They can do that, give us ideas," she told me.)

Juliet said out loud, "Okay, Michael, here's your chance. I'm in a jam. I've got to get up to the cathedral and I'm running late. Surely in all of Manhattan, you can find *one* cab that's empty!"

Within minutes, a free cab pulled up and she hopped in. Now Juliet grew up near New York City and had been in hundreds of cabs. She always looked at the dashboard for the driver's photos of his children or wife, or little images of saints, Jesus, or the Virgin Mary that are commonly fastened to the dash. But in all her years, she had never seen anything like what greeted her that evening. Stuck onto the dashboard was a cheap plastic statue of a winged form that bore the words THE RIGHT ARCHANGEL MICHAEL. And it was huge.

For a moment, Juliet couldn't speak. This was too weird—even synchronicity seemed unable to explain this incredible "coincidence."

The driver was named Tony, according to the license visible on the dash. Finding her voice, Juliet stammered, "Tony, tell me, what are you doing with the archangel Michael here in your cab?"

Tony turned to her and said, "Lady, let me tell you, he's a special friend of mine—he's my best friend, Mike!"

"Your friend *Mike?*"

"You don't know about Mike? Hey, he's the greatest! Let me tell you, my wife, she gets mad at me, she throws the spaghetti across the kitchen or whatever, I call on Mike and ask him, how do you handle women? The kids get in trouble in school, I call on Mike. I can't pay the rent, I call on Mike. I really recommend him to you—he can do anything! Of *course* I have him in my cab. Who else would I have?"

All the way to 110th Street and Amsterdam Avenue, Juliet heard a lecture on the virtues of the archangel Michael, and why he was Tony's best and greatest friend. At St. John the Divine, she got out and paid Tony, and he drove off, his statue of Michael like a guiding beacon on the dash.

Juliet said to herself, "All right, Juliet, you asked for a message, and now you've got to keep your promise." She was determined to keep up her end of the deal, despite some trepidation about the response of ecclesiastical authorities to a message that angels are real.

Inside the cathedral, she asked a docent what angel or angels guarded it. One graced the roof, but she didn't know its identity.

"The archangel Michael watches over this cathedral," the docent told her.

The answer was hardly a surprise.

The following night at the conclusion of the

conference—a huge success—Juliet said her little piece about how angels are not just pretty Renaissance paintings but are real and desire to help humanity. But they cannot do so unless humans ask for their help.

Nobody fainted away in horror at the idea. In fact, for weeks afterward, Juliet received an avalanche of mail, more than she had ever received in her life. The letters were testimonies of people's own beliefs and experiences with angels. "They *are* real!" was the overall enthusiastic response.

I asked Juliet how that experience changed her belief about angels.

"I didn't know they had such a sense of humor," she replied. "I felt the archangel himself was getting such a kick out of what was going on in that cab."

Juliet was also struck by the sense of sadness or loneliness about the figure of light that appeared in her room. "It seemed that the angels are hungry for communication with the human condition," she said. "Think of all the things a lifetime can bring—tragedy, heartbreak—and they would like to bring us hope. But it's like they're saying, 'Nobody's asked us to the party.'"

Juliet continues to call on angels for help "day and night," as she described it. "I feel very close to them, I talk to them. If I didn't believe in the angel kingdom, I'd never be doing what I'm doing now—there would be no Temple of Understanding. I'm not alone in this—there's something far wiser helping me out. I have friends, pals." She added somewhat wistfully, "But I haven't had any experience quite like that since."

To Test Our Character

Sometimes God sends angels among us, disguised as humans, to test us. The Bible tells us, in Genesis 18, that when Abraham was camped on the plains of Mamre, three men appeared before his tent. He welcomed the strangers and refreshed them with food and drink. Abraham was informed that Sarah, his wife, would bear a son. The idea seemed preposterous, for both Abraham and Sarah were quite old, and Sarah had never had children. Soon she bore a son, Isaac.

In 1946, Ruth Beck, of North Hollywood, California, was visited by a mysterious stranger one day as she was about to leave her house.

"My three children, ages ten, eight, and seven years, were waiting for me in the car," she recalled. "I had to close the doors and turn the lights off. Just as I turned the kitchen light off, I heard a knock on the front door. Thinking it was one of the children playing a prank on me, I opened the door. Standing in front of me, to my surprise, was a very tall, handsome stranger. He was very clean, clothes were pressed, all in black. I took special notice that he wore a cloak with a shoulder-length cape effect.

"He smiled and said, 'Could you give me something to eat? I've been on the road two days and have a long way yet to go.'

"Startled, I thought, 'I'm in a hurry.' Then I pondered, 'What shall I give him?' There were just two eggs in the icebox. I hurriedly scrambled them, and buttered two slices of bread, and made a nice sandwich. I put wax paper around it and put it in a paper bag. I added hot coffee to a bit of milk in the milk carton, then put it in a thick white mug, and took it all out to him. He smiled and thanked me.

"Then I turned the lights out and went to join the children in the car. They said, 'What took you so long?' I replied, 'Why, didn't you see, I fed that man on the porch.' They said, 'What man?'

"He would have had to pass the car twice to get on the porch. I said, 'Let's go look.' They hopped out of the car, and we all stood a few paces from the car. It wasn't dark yet. There were no trees, houses, or anything to obstruct our view. We could see no one!

"I believe God sent this to me as a test to see if I were too much in a hurry to stop and assist one in need. I also believe that someday, as a token of remembrance, the cup will be returned to me."

These are but a few of the ways that angels enter our world. No two experiences are ever the same. Yet we ascribe such experiences to the same agents, angels. What are the factors that have shaped our belief in these beings?

2

Between Heaven and Earth

Spiritual beings who inhabit a plane of existence between the human and the divine—this is an ancient concept common to many religions and cultures. The angel as it is popularly depicted is a crossbreed descended from the unearthly entities of Babylonian, Persian, Egyptian, Sumerian, and Greek faiths. Its popular image as a heavenly messenger is generally limited to monotheistic religions that divide the cosmos into heaven, earth, and hell, requiring couriers to shuttle back and forth between the divisions. This particular brand of angel originated in Persia's Zoroastrian faith and was then handed down to Judaism, Christianity, and Islam.

The word angel itself is a mutation of the Greek *angelos,* a translation of the Persian word "angaros," or "courier." The Hebrew term is *mal'akh,* meaning "messenger" or "envoy." Even this definition is ambiguous, for "messenger" or "envoy" is used in five different senses in the Bible. It can mean:

1) the Word, given by God to the world
2) St. John the Baptist, the precursor of the Messiah
3) priests, who act as God's ambassadors to people
4) prophets
5) angels

Generally, the term *messenger* or *envoy* is used in the Scriptures to mean angels. But acting as messenger is only one of their functions, and these enlightened spirits can be found worldwide, throughout history, playing many roles.

History of the Angel

How old is the concept of the angel? Images of supernatural winged creatures have been found in ancient Mesopotamia and Sumeria. The Assyrians had their *karibu* (the source of the word *cherubim*), which were fierce, winged beasts possessing features both animal and human. The role of the angel as protector can perhaps be traced to these ancestors, which acted as temple guards in Babylon and Sumeria.

The Greeks made a big contribution to angel lore with their gods, such as Hermes, the winged messenger. Hermes is often credited as being the source of archangel Michael. (Many of the Greek gods were molded into angels by the Church in its attempt to convert the pagans.) The Greeks also had *daimones*, spirits who came in both good and evil forms, the good ones being protectors. Socrates spoke of his daimon, who constantly whispered in his ear. Daimones evolved into "demons" in Christianization, and in the process they lost their good-natured brethren.

The Aryans who came to India and Persia around 2500 B.C. believed in *devas* (meaning "shining ones"), who were deities subordinate to their supreme god, Dyeus. Perhaps it was from them that angels inherited their most salient characteristic—the ability to shine, or radiate light. The "el" suffix so common in angels' names is understood in several languages to mean "shining" or "radiant."

The devas made their way into the *Veda,* a collection of early sacred Hindu writings, where they were depicted in a hierarchical (but still polytheistic) arrangement. According to the *Veda,* devas existed in the three worlds—earth, heaven, and a spiritual realm in between. They were closely aligned with the elements of nature—fire, water, earth, and air—which were considered expressions of their existence. Devas of water, for example, were assigned the feminine role of caretakers, or nourishers, of all living things.

Devas also found their way into Zoroastrianism, the religion founded by the prophet Zoroaster (Zarathustra) in sixth-century Persia. It was through Zoroastrianism that devas evolved into angels. In founding this monotheistic faith, Zoroaster rejected the pantheism of the Hindus and offered instead a single, supreme deity, Ahura Mazda, locked in an eternal struggle against his evil enemy Ahaitin. Mazda is aided in this struggle by the good deeds of humans. He is also aided by seven archangels, the *amesha spenta,* who are the gods of Babylon and Assyria recycled into roles more appropriate to a monotheistic religion. They represent the concepts of wisdom, truth, immortality, deserved good luck, piety, salvation, and obedience. Each angel also acts as the guardian of something—fire, for example. *Yazatas* are another breed of Zoroastrian angels and, like the devas before them, they rule the elements.

Zoroaster's brand of angels took hold and was handed down to Judaism, Christianity, and finally Islam. Islam's *malaika* (again, "messengers") are androgynous beings made of light who act as guardians of humans. Their names and personalities are borrowed from Judeo-Christian angels—for example, Mika'il (Michael) and Djibril (Gabriel).

Judeo-Christian Angels

Zoroastrianism was popular during the Hebrews' captivity in Persia and made its mark on biblical writings. While Judaism did not allow for any gods other than Yahweh, the idea of angelic intermediaries to God was acceptable and adoptable.

Angels appear as guides to heaven in the Jewish Kabbalah, writings containing mystical knowledge that is passed on to those advanced enough to comprehend it. There are also ten beings called *sefirot*, which are composed of the energy of God and are known as Grace, Wisdom, Splendor, Understanding, Knowledge, Foundation, Eternity, Power, Beauty, and Crown. They stand together to form a tree—the Tree of Life.

At the top of the tree is Metatron, the angel of the Lord. He is considered in some accounts to be the greatest of the angels—there is scarcely an angelic duty or function that is not related to him. Metatron also is the representative of God who led the tribes of Israel through the wilderness, and probably is the dark angel who wrestled with Jacob. He is sometimes identified with Satan. In Judaic literature, the principle name of Satan is Samael, (also spelled Sammael), which means "poison angel."

The etymology of Metatron is unclear. Possibly the name itself was intended to be a secret and may have been produced through a glossolalia type of altered state of consciousness. Glossolalia is speaking in tongues, and is perhaps best known for its part in charismatic religions. Metatron is sometimes called the Prince of the Countenance, meaning he is the chief angel of those angels who are privileged to look upon the countenance of God.

Descriptions of him tell of a spirit or pillar of fire with thirty-six pairs of wings and myriad eyes. His face is more dazzling than the sun. He serves as God's angel of death, instructing Gabriel and Samael which human souls to take at any given moment.

Enoch's Seven Heavens

We might think that the Bible would inform us about the origin, nature, and functions of angels, but it falls far short of the task. In fact, the Bible is rather vague on the subject, mentioning angels or alluding to them without offering much in the way of specifics. Only two angels are mentioned by name: Michael ("who is as God"), and Gabriel ("God is my strength"). The Apocrypha mentions others, most notably Raphael ("the shining one who heals") and Uriel ("fire of God"). According to the Book of

Revelation, in the New Testament, there are seven archangels who stand before God, but we are left to guess at the identities of the others.

Most of the angel lore that has been handed down through the centuries comes from the Apocrypha ("hidden books") and pseudepigrapha (Apocalyptic books), writings that were declared heretical by the church for one reason or another. The apocryphal Book of Tobit tells a great deal about the archangel Raphael (see chapter nine). It is the Chronicles of Enoch, part of the pseudepigrapha, that tell us the most about angels in general.

According to legend, Enoch was a prophet so spiritually advanced that God had angels take him directly to heaven to record what he saw. Indeed, Enoch became a frequent flyer to heaven, and he recorded his travels there in detail. His experiences enlightened him so much that God turned him into the angel Metatron.

Most likely, the Chronicles of Enoch were written by numerous anonymous authors around the first and second centuries A.D. The Chronicles were denounced in the fourth century A.D. by St. Jerome. One of the chief objections to them was that they portray a multilayered heaven that contains hell, populated by fallen angels. The concept of hell within heaven apparently was too much for early church authorities.

Enoch's accounts are compelling reading. According to the story, Enoch was 365 years old when two angels appeared and whisked him off to heaven.

Enoch remained in heaven for sixty days. He recorded what he saw in 366 books, which were handed down to his sons. After a hiatus back on earth of thirty days, Enoch was once again transported to heaven, where God immortalized him as Metatron, installing him in the seventh heaven.

Enoch's heavenly adventures began one day when he was asleep on his couch. A "great distress" came into his heart, which he could not understand. Two beings appeared before him, which he described as men:

"And there appeared to me two men, exceedingly big, so that I never saw such on earth; their faces were shining like the sun, their eyes too *were* like a burning light, and from their lips was fire coming forth with clothing and singing of various kinds in appearance purple, their wings *were* brighter than gold, their hands whiter than snow."

Enoch was frightened, but the angels assured him that he should not fear—they had been sent by God to take him into heaven. They bore him up on their wings to the clouds to the first heaven. In all, Enoch found seven heavens and seven corresponding earths, all united to each other by hooks. Beyond the seventh heaven lay three more heavens.

The first heaven, ruled by Gabriel, is the one closest to Earth, and contains the winds and the clouds. The angels who live here are astronomers and rule the stars and heavenly bodies. There also are angels who are guardians of ice, snow, flowers, and dew.

The second heaven is ruled by Raphael and is a dark penal area where fallen angels await judgment. His guiding angels, said Enoch, "showed me darkness, and there I saw prisoners hanging, watched, awaiting the great and boundless judgment, and these angels were dark-looking, more than earthly darkness, and incessantly making weeping through all hours."

Enoch was told that these prisoners were "God's

apostates," fallen angels who had turned away from God with their prince, who was fastened in the fifth heaven.

The fallen angels asked Enoch to pray for them. He wondered how he, a mere mortal man, could pray for angels. And if he did so, then who would pray for him? (This idea of angels begging for the mercy of a mortal perhaps contributed to the expulsion of the Chronicles of Enoch from canonical literature.)

The third heaven is ruled by Anahel and is a land of contrasts. One part of this heaven, the northern section, is actually hell, ice cold and sulfurous, filled with torturing angels who punish the evil souls who reside there. The condemned include those who dishonor God, sin against nature, and practice enchantments and witchcraft. However, the rest of this heaven is an Eden-like garden where manna is made and the souls of the holy—those who are righteous and compassionate—reside. Angels of light watch over this heaven.

The fourth heaven, under the jurisdiction of archangel Michael, contains Holy Jerusalem and its temple, all made of gold, surrounded by rivers made of milk, honey, wine, and oil. The Tree of Life is to be found in this heaven, as well as the sun and the moon. Here Enoch heard the singing of angels:

"In the midst of the heavens I saw armed soldiers, serving the Lord, with tympana and organs, with incessant voice, with sweet voice, with sweet and incessant *voice* and various singing, which is impossible to describe, and *which* astonishes every mind, so wonderful and marvelous is the singing of those angels, and I was delighted listening to it."

The fifth heaven is yet another prison, a fiery ravine

where the angelic Watchers, or Grigori, are being imprisoned for marrying into the human race (see "Rebel Angels" later in this chapter).

The sixth heaven is full of scholarly angels, studying astronomy, nature, and *homo sapiens.* Here Enoch found archangels, as well as angels who rule over all the cycles and functions of nature—the seasons, the calendar, the rivers and seas, the fruits of the earth, the grass, etc. There also are angels who record all the lives and deeds of every human soul, to set forth before God.

In the seventh heaven, Enoch found the higher angels, such as the thrones, cherubim, seraphim, and dominions, as well as "fiery troops of great archangels." These angelic host bowed down before the Lord, singing his praises.

Enoch's two angel guides left him at the end of the seventh heaven. He was terrified, but Gabriel appeared before him, caught him up as though a leaf caught up by wind, and transported him higher.

In the eighth heaven, called Muzaloth, Enoch saw the "changer of the seasons, of drought, and of wet, and of the twelve signs of the zodiac." The ninth heaven, called Kuchavim, holds the heavenly homes of the twelve signs of the zodiac.

Then archangel Michael escorted Enoch to the tenth heaven, where he beheld the face of God. It was, said Enoch, "like iron made to glow in fire, and brought out, emitting sparks, and it burns.

"Thus I saw the Lord's face, but the Lord's face is ineffable, marvelous and very awful, and very, very terrible. . . .

"And I cannot tell the quantity of his many instructions, and various voices, the Lord's throne very great and not made with hands, nor the quantity of those standing round him, troops of cherubim and seraphim, nor their incessant singing, nor his immutable beauty, and who shall tell of the ineffable greatness of his glory?"

God instructed Michael to "take Enoch from out of his earthly garments, and anoint him with my sweet ointment, and put him into the garments of my Glory." Enoch then took on a shining appearance, like the angels around him. God summoned the archangel Pravuil, "whose knowledge was quicker in wisdom than the other archangels, who wrote all the deeds of the Lord," to bring out the books of knowledge for Enoch to read.

After instruction from Pravuil, Enoch wrote his 366 books in thirty days. He was then summoned by the Lord, who revealed to him the creation story, and that the world would end on the eighth day of creation (or after 8,000 years), when time would cease. Enoch was given all the rules of morality and righteousness for humans to live by.

After these revelations, Enoch was sent back to the earth for thirty days, so that he could pass on the teachings to his sons and others. God then took Enoch back into heaven.

The Angelic Hierarchy

Just as the Judeo-Christian concept of the cosmos is hierarchical, so is the arrangement of angelic beings that inhabit it. But the borders seem to blur, as angels sometimes occupy more than one position and play multiple roles simultaneously. For example, before the fall, Satan (Lucifer) was the ruler of the seraphim, the highest order of angels; at the same time, he was also considered an archangel, a position much lower on the totem pole.

The best-known hierarchy derives from the two main sources of information on the subject: Pseudo-Dionysius's *Celestial Hierarchies* and Saint Thomas Aquinas's *Summa Theologica.*

Pseudo-Dionysius, also known as Dionysius the Areopagite, is a mysterious Greek figure credited with authoring some rather dense but enduring theological and philosophical tracts. The name is a pseudonym, and the real identity of the person writing under it is unknown. Moreover, the exact dates of his writings are unknown as well, although it is believed that they date to the fifth or sixth centuries A.D. The works were influential for medieval Christian thinkers, including Saint Thomas Aquinas (1225–1274), one of the great theologians of the Middle Ages.

Whoever he was, Pseudo-Dionysius followed the Platonic and Neoplatonic pattern of three. He conceived of all reality in triadic hierarchies. In *Celestial Hierarchies,* he presents an angelic kingdom divided into three realms, each containing three orders, each further broken down into three levels of intelligences. In each group of three, the function of the first level is perfection or union; of the second level, it is illumination; of the third level, purification. This triadic arrangement provides a means for the divine, or spirit, to descend into matter, and for matter to ascend to divinity.

A hierarchy, said Pseudo-Dionysius, is "a sacred order, a state of understanding and an activity approximating as closely as possible to the divine." The goal of a hierarchy "is to enable beings to be as like as possible to God and to be at one with him." Thus, through the angelic hierarchy, humankind has a way of reaching up to God and sharing in the light that emanates from him.

Pseudo-Dionysius said that angels are nearer to God than are humans, "since their participation in him takes so many forms." He elaborated,

Their thinking processes imitate the divine. They look on the divine likeness with a transcendent eye. They model their intellects on him. Hence it is natural for them to enter into a more generous communion with the Deity, because they are forever marching toward the heights, because, as permitted, they are drawn to a concentration of an unfailing love for God, because they immaterially receive undiluted the original enlightenment, and because, ordered by such enlightenment, theirs is a life of total intelligence. They have the first and most diverse participation in the divine, and they, in turn, provide the first and most diverse revelations of the divine hiddenness. That is why they have a preeminent right to the title of angel or messenger, since it is they who first are granted the divine enlightenment and it is they who pass on to us these revelations which are so far beyond us.

At the center of the triadic angel kingdom is God, emitting rapid vibrations that slow as they move out from the source and become light. As the vibrations slow, they become heat and finally matter. Nine orders of celestial beings surround God, divided, as mentioned, into three triads. At any level, the higher angels possess all the powers of those lower, but not those of any higher level.

The upper triad is composed of seraphim (love), cherubim (knowledge), and thrones. The entities of the upper triad are in direct contact with God. They receive "the primal theophanies and perfections," said Pseudo-Dionysius, which they pass on to the middle triad. The middle triad consists of dominions, powers, and virtues. They in turn pass the word to the last triad, which is home to principalities, archangels, and finally angels. This last triad is responsible for communicating God's word to humans.

The levels of angels are:

Seraphim. Their name means "fire makers" or "carriers of warmth." The seraphim set up the vibration of love, which in turn creates the field of life. These angels are of such subtlety that they rarely are perceived by human consciousness. When they so choose, they can manifest in a humanlike form with four heads and six wings—two for flying, two to cover the face, and two to cover the feet. They are able to shed their skin and appear in their true, brilliant form. For this reason, seraphim are often identified with the serpent or dragon, which in various mythologies are described as brilliant flying lights in the sky.

Enoch declared that there are only four seraphim, one for each direction.

Cherubim. The name comes from the Hebrew "kerub," which means either "fullness of knowledge" or "one who intercedes." Their name, said Pseudo-Dionysius, "signifies the power to know and see God, to receive the greatest gifts of his light, to contemplate the divine splendor in primordial power, to be filled with the gifts that bring wisdom and to share these generously with subordinates as a part of the beneficent outpouring of wisdom." Cherubs have four faces and four wings. They also function as charioteers to God.

Thrones. Also known as "ophanim" and "galgallin," these creatures function as the actual chariots driven by the cherubs. They are depicted as great wheels containing many eyes, and reside in the area of the cosmos where material form begins to take shape. They chant glorias to God and remain forever in his presence.

Dominions. Dominions (also known as "dominations," "lords," and "kuriotetes"), according to Pseudo-Dionysius, regulate the duties of the angels. According to others, they function as "channels of mercy."

Powers. Also called "potentiates," "dynamis," and "authorities," these angels act as patrols, on the watch for demons trying to exert their evil influence. While they work to maintain a balance between good and evil, they themselves can be either good or evil. Camael is the ruler of the powers, and while he is considered to be a favored angel he is also known as the duke of hell. Either way, he rules 144,000 angels of vengeance and death. Powers also moonlight as spirit guides to the deceased who have lost their way.

Virtues. These beings are in charge of miracles and of providing courage, and are sometimes referred to as "the shining ones" or the "brilliant ones."

Principalities. These beings watch over the actions of the earth's nations and cities, and inspire leaders to make the right decisions. They are also in charge of religion on this planet.

Archangels. Archangels are a busy lot: they are liaisons between God and mortals; they are in charge of heaven's armies in the battle against hell, and they are the supervisors of the guardian angels.

Michael is the most famous of the archangels and the only one named as an archangel in the Bible. He is said to be the angel who defeated Satan and hurled him into hell, and who will return with the keys to hell in order to lock him up for one thousand years. Michael is usually depicted carrying a sword and possessing "many-eyed" wings—that is, covered in peacock feathers. He possesses many of the attributes of Mercury/Hermes, given to him by the church in its attempts to convert the worshipers of that god. For example, he is known as the spirit guide of the dead, a job inherited from Mercury.

Other angels have been accorded the rank of archangel. Gabriel is the angel of annunciation, resurrection, mercy, and death, and is the angel who appeared to Mary to inform her of her unusual pregnancy. Gabriel is said to guide the soul from paradise to the womb and there instruct it for the nine months prior to birth. He has 140 pairs of wings and is said to sit at the left of God.

Raphael's name originates from the Hebrew *rapha,* which means healer or doctor; thus Rapha-el is "the shining one who heals." As such, he is often connected with the symbol of healing, the serpent. He is entrusted with the physical well-being of the earth and its human inhabitants, and is said to be the friendliest of the angels. However, he can also appear in the form of a monster and behave in a demoniacal manner.

Uriel is a punishing angel—the one who stands

with fiery sword at the gates of Eden. He also punished Moses for not circumcising his son. But Uriel is not without a compassionate side. He is said to have given the Kabbalah to humanity and to have warned Noah of the coming flood.

Angels. The class of higher beings closest to the material world are the angels. They are the true couriers of the heavens, delivering the messages of God to humans. Angels also have a reputation as the musicians of the cosmos. The vibrations of their music are more spiritual impulses than sound waves; thus it is not heard by humans as music but experienced as moods and inspirations.

Rebel Angels

To err may be human, but apparently we aren't the only ones capable of making bad decisions. Most angel lore contains stories of angels gone bad. According to the Bible, one-third of Heaven's legion fell from grace—figuratively, and according to some legends, literally.

As previously mentioned, Enoch witnessed a penal colony in the fifth heaven where gigantic angels known as the Grigori (or Watchers, or Those Who Sleep Not) are kept prisoner. As the story goes, about two hundred of the Watchers were living up to their name—watching over the earth—and found themselves watching the female descendants of Adam and Eve with more than brotherly love on their minds. They finally decided to disobey God, descend to the earth, and take the women as wives. This act had many problematic consequences. To begin with, it was a sin of hubris—a mixture of pride and lust. It also resulted in a mixing of the spiritual with the material, which was strictly forbidden as far as God was concerned. And the Watchers imparted to their wives angelic knowledge not meant to be shared with humans—secrets on growing herbs, working with minerals, working "enchantments," etc.

Worse still, the union between the fallen angels and the daughters of Eve resulted in very unnatural offspring. These nephilim, or "fallen ones," were gigantic, destructive creatures. They required great amounts of food, and when it ran out they would eat humans and even each other. The purpose of the great flood was to eliminate these abnormal beings and preserve the human race. However, there was a second occurrence of these creatures in Canaan, and Israel was charged with destroying them. The destruction was incomplete, and many got away, their fate unknown.

The fate of the watchers themselves was to be held prisoner forever. Their leader, Azazel, was cast by Raphael into a dark pit (either on earth or in the fifth heaven) and remains there until Judgment Day, when he will be cast into the fire.

It is free will that seems to get some angels into trouble. Another legend of the fall tells of a war between free-willed angels, some who were fortified by the grace of God and some who were on their own. Not surprisingly, those with God's extra shot of grace, led by archangel Michael, defeated the army of 133 million and cast them down to hell.

Saint Thomas Aquinas stated that the angels' only opportunity for free will is at the time of their creation, and even then, they always choose God.

However, the Gnostics (discussed later in more detail) believed that, in exercising their free will, angels naturally drifted away from God. The angels who drifted the least stayed in the astral plane; those who drifted the farthest became demons.

The most infamous of the rebel angels was, of course, Lucifer, the bringer of light turned prince of darkness, who is usually credited with leading the other angels in the big fall. Lucifer is identified as Satan (from the heavenly office of *ha-satan,* or adversary), who, while still in the heavens, appeared to hold more than one position in the hierarchy simultaneously. Similarly, he possessed a multitude of aliases and personalities—Metatron is one. But most share the same basic life story: the most glorified of the angels, most beloved of God, made a colossal blunder of pride and was condemned forever to a dark, embittered existence. He lost his luminous quality and inherited the goatlike features of his randy Greek ancestor, Pan.

Perhaps the cause of Satan's exile was his refusal to bow to Adam when God presented him to the angels. One legend has it that Satan refused to bow because he had been previously instructed to bow to no one but God, in which case he was just obeying orders. Perhaps he refused to bow to any but God because of his deep love for the Creator. Or perhaps he was simply jealous of God's creation, which would explain why he's spent his entire postfall life trying to separate humankind from God. Regardless, he was flung into hell, and one-third of the angels followed him.

In another incarnation, as Shaher, the Morning Star, he was the last star to leave the sky before the sun rose. One morning, his pride got the best of him and he tried to overcome the rising sun; for this act of insubordination he was expelled from heaven.

Gnostic Angelology

The Gnostics were a mystical Christian sect that flourished in the second century. They believed that matter is evil and that freedom comes from *gnosis,* or spiritual truth. The church considered them heretical, and persecuted and purged them accordingly.

One of their acts of heresy was disagreeing over the Judeo-Christian theory of creation. Gnostics say there is no singular, higher being who created the world. Rather, there is an all-encompassing divine spirit that divided itself, creating various worlds and beings, human and spiritual, in the process. One of these was the female principal Sophia, who represented the concept of wisdom (and whose name is Greek for wisdom). Other emanations from the source included the concepts of love, power, truth, and mercy. These formless concepts eventually solidified into angelic beings.

At one point, the divine source withdrew itself from these beings and gave them the free will to stay or to go. Some chose to remain close to the source, serving it and aiding those humans who desire reunion with the divine. Others—the "fallen" angels—became so alienated from the source that they grew arrogant, all claiming themselves to be the one and only. According to the Gnostics, the Creator who is worshipped in Judeo-Christian religions is actually one of these arrogant fallen angels. Satan falsely claimed to be the creator and ruler of the cosmos, and he was believed.

Angelic Beings in Other Religions

Even religions and cultures that do not embrace the Judeo-Christian concept of angels believe in spiritual beings who act as mentors and guardians.

While the angels of Western religions are a species genetically distinct from humans, the divine beings of Eastern religions are often humans who have reached a high rung on the karmic ladder. For example, Buddhists and Hindus do not believe in angels as bearers of great truths; rather, they have wise humans who fulfill this function. Buddhist devas are mortal beings who have earned a place in the astral plane not accessible by regular human beings; however, being mortal, they are subject to the laws of reincarnation. (On the other hand, devas can also be defined as nature spirits that sometimes come to the aid of deserving humans.)

In Mahayana Buddhism we find the "bodhisattva," who are one step beyond the enlightened bodhi. Bodhisattva are humans who have attained not only enlightenment but also total compassion. They reside between heaven and earth and, like the deva, must also pass through the cycle of reincarnation. The spiritual energy within them is referred to as a *dakini*, or angel. Bodhisattva act in the usual angelic capacity toward humans, teaching and healing; they also guide the spirits of the dying.

But a few superhuman beings do pop up in the Eastern faiths. There are *devis*, for example, which represent the feminine form of God. Devis are used when the Creator wishes to communicate with a human. They are filled with *shaktis,* the energies of God. The Taoists have their immortals, former humans who have attained physical immortality and status as demigods. They fulfill the usual angelic duties of healing, protecting, and delivering messages. The Hindus believe in birdlike *apsaras,* which carry the dead into paradise. And there are the *kinpuru'sh,* winged creatures that remain close to God at all times.

Candomblé (a form of Santería) is a Brazilian religion, adopted from Africa, that emphasizes communion with nature as the path to guidance and enlightenment. According to this faith, we can receive truth and wisdom by approaching the spirits of nature with an attitude of humility and good intentions. The angels of this religion are known as *orishas.* Orishas are immaterial beings who act as helpers to Olorún, the god of Candomblé, and each is aligned with an element of nature, much like the Hindu devas. Chango, for example, is the orisha of thunder, and Oshoun is the orisha of romantic love and fertility. They make up a family of over four hundred members, with Oshalá as the father of orishas and Yemanja as the mother.

The energy of the orishas is dualistic; thus, there are both male and female spirits. At birth everyone receives a male and a female orisha, which behave in the manner of guardian angels. In order to discover the identities of one's orishas and receive their guidance, a person must go to a "power spot," a place in nature where one feels most at peace and attuned to the cosmos. When a person intuitively discovers power spots, he or she discovers the home of the personal orishas, and it is there that their guidance can best be received.

Native Americans have angellike creatures in animal form, spirits who sometimes help people and deliver messages from above. The shamans, in their visits to the underworld, are accompanied by animal spirit guides. And many Indian cultures believe that the spirits of their ancestors act as guardian angels to the living.

The Celtic peoples have their fairies, sprites, elves, brownies, and leprechauns. The stories of their origin are many, but one legend claims that they are the angels who fell with Satan. Djinn are elflike spirits of Arabian origin, some friendly, some not. They are recognized as beings of a substance other than human. However, like fairies, leprechauns, and the other sprites to which they are related, fun and mischief are their domain. They do not possess the spiritual clout of angels.

Cycles of Popularity

Angels reached a height of popularity during the Middle Ages. They experienced an explosion in population and power, being everywhere and protecting all things, and their estimated numbers soared to over 300 million.

But what goes up must come down—even angels—and various historical events contributed to their loss in popularity. The Inquisition focused attention away from the angels and toward their dark brethren of the pit. And the Black Plague diminished people's faith in celestial protectors.

By the end of the Renaissance, interest in angels was at a low point as spiritual contemplation was replaced by a new focus on science. The Age of Enlightenment arrived. Knowledge, formerly a privilege of the church, became more available through the invention of the printing press. Astronomical discoveries put the earth in its place—a minuscule dot in an overwhelmingly large cosmos. Angels began to disappear from serious discussion, and in the art world they were replaced, strangely enough, by pagan gods.

The Protestant Reformation of the sixteenth century rejected the Christian angel hierarchy, with the exception of the fallen angels and their leader. John Calvin denounced the consideration of angels as a waste of time. Martin Luther, while admitting to their existence, suggested that they be kept in perspective and certainly not be considered divine.

The church has repeatedly vacillated on the subject of angels. Saint Paul denounced the worship of angels, and although in 325 angels became "official" in the church, in 343 the worship of them was frowned upon. By the end of the eighth century, archangels were accepted to a limited extent, and their names and duties agreed upon.

Today the church still tends to sweep angels under the carpet, stressing that worship should be restricted to God and not include God's messengers. The church does foster belief, however, in the guardian angel (see chapter 4).

Angels Today

Angels have survived the inevitable peaks and valleys in their popularity. While the age of science and information may have pushed angels aside temporarily, they are reappearing as we now shift our focus away from Technology as the answer. The "New Age" is gradually forcing us to look to alternative dimensions for answers—be it through hypnosis, yoga, meditation, or channeling—and we need experienced guides to help.

The shining ones in our lives today have manifested as spirit guides—on both sides of the grave. Many people accept the presence of higher intellects who keep watch over their lives, guiding and protecting; these range from the spirits of the dead to abstract concepts of a higher self. In the phenomenon of near-death experience, the "dead" encounter creatures of light who act as guides in the astral plane. The fascinating accounts of UFO witnesses and those who claim to have had encounters with extraterrestrials often feature descriptions remarkably like the angelic descriptions of old. They also bear great resemblance to the angelic beings known as Shining Ones, who first appeared in Lebanon about ten thousand years ago. They were tall, with huge, bright eyes, and faces that glowed with an unearthly, luminous quality. Shining Ones were also seen in Tibet and in Sumeria, where they came down in fiery craft, "commingled" with human women, and offered lessons in agriculture—much like the lusty Grigori.

And, as always, we still hear the simple tales of people in distress receiving help from mysterious strangers—unknown humans or animals—which then go on their way, never to be seen again.

Why We Believe

What fuels our belief in angels? Are they a favorite fairy tale that refuses to die? Are they, as Carl Jung would suggest, archetypal images from a collective imagination, buried in the primitive, "reptilian" layer of our brains, which in times of great stress appear in our neocortex as reality? Are they, as some suggest, visions witnessed during out-of-body experiences (OBE) of the ethereal bodies of others who are also experiencing OBE? Are they energies representing the life force, representing our own psychic or higher selves, onto which we project form, making them easier for us to comprehend? Or is it their function as guardians that makes them so universally and time-lessly appealing—a security blanket that we can't quite give up?

For a while now we have been glib, educated sophisticates of the age of scientific progress, looking upon angels as the quaint folklore of the ignorant and the "religious." But as we begin to focus on the spiritual—the "higher self"—we are finding that the angels are still around, and that they are better informed than we are.

As Michael Grosso points out in his essay, "The Cult of the Guardian Angel" (in *Angels and Mortals),* this rising popularity reflects our turning away from science and toward the primal, or barbarian, imagination: "In these new barbarian times, the gods and goddesses, the demons and fairies, the griffins and guardian angels we have trampled under the feet of scientific rationalism are returning with a vengeance."

3

The Changing Image of Angels

As noted in chapter 2, the ancient Middle Eastern predecessors of the angels were imposing beasts, pillars of ferocious strength. Somehow angels were transformed into floating beings composed of ethereal light.

Angels gradually lost their beastly forms and became humanoid. Female bodies borrowed from the goddess religions dominated at first, but eventually the angels became distinctly male in form. They lacked wings or halos, and appeared to look just like mortal men.

Early Bible tales of angels depicted them as wingless and rather earthy and humanoid. The three strangers who enjoyed Abraham's hospitality seemed quite unremarkable until they returned the favor by making his elderly wife fertile. The manlike angel found sitting inside Christ's tomb was also wingless.

However, in 560 B.C. the prophet Ezekiel had a spectacular close encounter with beings that were certainly not human. These winged creatures descended in a fiery cloud and had four faces each (human, ox, eagle, and lion). They moved on wheels and made a tremendous thundering noise. Encounters with angels of this type, particularly those arriving in fiery, wheeled craft, have fueled theories that angels are extraterrestrials.

Perhaps such encounters are responsible for the radiant qualities that developed in angel imagery. Halos and shining lights began to accompany them by the end of the fourth century. By the eighth century, the pagan gods and goddesses were again influencing their image, particularly the winged characters, such as Nike, Eros, and Hermes.

But their "fleshiness" returned with the Renaissance. During this period, focused as it was on science and the laws of nature ("reality") angels lost much of their ethereal, transparent quality and became again more solid. Some even lost their wings. Cherubs were reduced to chubby babies—Italian *putti*—an image that is still popular today. Angels were increasingly depicted as feminine, and those that were male were *clearly* male. If they had to lose their wings, at least they grew sex organs as compensation.

By the end of the Renaissance, artists, like the rest of society, began to lose interest in angels. Since then, they never managed to regain their strong foothold in the art world, and the angelic image established during the Renaissance has remained relatively untouched.

What Are Angels Made Of?

The substance (or lack of substance) of angels has been much debated through history. Some suggest that angels are naturally occurring energies and that if they seem to us to be visible and have form, it is because we are "seeing" them with the inner eye and projecting onto them a visible form that is entirely subjective.

Saint Thomas Aquinas (who held forth in great detail about angels in general, giving us a data base of angel information that still affects our image of angels today) declared that angels are intellect without substance. They are pure thought forms. However, they can take on a physical body if they wish and if it makes their jobs easier.

Swedish mystic Emanuel Swedenborg, in the eighteenth century, through personal communications with angels, discovered that angels have no material body and therefore cannot reflect light and be visible. They can be seen only if they take on a body temporarily, or if they are perceived through the inner eye, or third eye. (Swedenborg also claimed that angels were the souls of humans.) They are, however, capable of speech, according to Swedenborg.

Male? Female? Both?

Angels are most likely androgynous, representing the ideal union of male and female into one whole. The purpose of the Torah, according to the Hebrews, is to unite the female half of God (Shekinah, who was exiled after the fall of Adam and Eve) with the male God. Some propose that angels are able to participate (among themselves) in an act of love that, while similar to sex, is really more a spiritual intercourse—a total union of two souls. The church states that angels are immaterial and therefore do not have any reproductive abilities. It would also make sense that if they are immortal, reproduction is unnecessary.

Yet angels seem to be able to at least appear male or female. And the Watchers who mated with human women apparently possessed the physical wherewithal to do so. In Genesis 18, the three angels who come to Abraham sit down and eat. Whether or not the angels actually ate, or only appeared to eat, has been the subject of entire doctoral theses and ongoing debates in theological circles. In the apocryphal Book of Tobit, the archangel Raphael, who appeared as a man, told his human charges that he only gave the appearance of eating and drinking, causing them to have visions, in order to disguise his identity. Milton's angels of *Paradise Lost* were male (although they were able to be either sex) and were able to participate in all the physical functions of humans, including eating and having sex.

Sharon Chamberlain, of Santa Fe, Texas, related to me a vision she had of an angel:

"My experience happened following the time of the Harmonic Convergence in August 1988. I had given my promise to mankind in a very private meditation. With everything that I had heard about this event, I expected something unusual to happen. When nothing did, I felt that I had done something wrong. That my effort was in vain. It was shortly thereafter that this happened. I don't remember exactly how long—maybe a couple of weeks.

"I was lying on my back in bed when I awoke. My eyes, surprisingly, were already open when I realized the vision before me. It was hanging above my bed. I remember it so clearly. Especially the face. Its look was androgynous, but I felt that the gender was male. His features were plain and his skin pale. His hair was coarse blond with a layered look, but not too long. He was smiling at me.

"I thought that I might be having a narcoleptic seizure or something, but I leaned up on one arm to get closer. I asked him what he wanted. He just continued to smile at me. Maybe I should have asked him something different, because shortly after that he disappeared, leaving me staring at the ceiling.

"I never felt frightened or upset. My demeanor was calm and serene. I lay back in bewilderment, wondering what it was all about. I never doubted what I saw."

Sometimes angels simply look in on us and let us know they are present. In Sharon's case, the angel seemed to be doing just that, as well as giving her a sign that her Harmonic Convergence meditation had been significant.

I had a similar experience myself in the early 1980s, before I began to recognize and communicate with the angelic presences around me. The vision occurred shortly after my father's death. I spent a lot of time thinking about the afterlife, and reading books in pursuit of spiritual insight. One quiet Sunday evening, I was engaged in such reading in the living room of the house we were occupying then, in the suburbs in

Westchester County, New York. At some point, my attention was distracted by a mysterious light outside that kept moving slowly back and forth, crossing a window and going toward the front door, which was glass. It was small and round, and orange in color.

I stopped reading to watch the light cross the window pane and head for the door. I looked at the glass door, waiting for it to show up. I was puzzled what it was. Suddenly I realized that a face was looking in on me, framed in the glass door. Several things hit me all at once: a person was at the door—but wait, the dogs didn't bark—good heavens, there was no body attached to the face! It was pale and androgynous, but I had the impression that it was masculine. It was serene and peaceful, and just seemed to be presenting itself for my awareness. It was gone within seconds. I've always though that it was an angel, giving me a glimpse of what lies in alternate realities.

Our Own Perceptions

All of these changing perceptions of angels show how we ourselves mold their image. Angels are vibrations of love and light—they are truly formless. In order for us to be able to perceive them, and to comprehend them, we ourselves project shape, features, and identities onto them. We are best able to relate to angels as humanlike beings. They reveal themselves to us in a manner fitting the circumstances and needs of the moment. For example, Joan of Arc perceived the archangel Michael as clothed in golden armor. How appropriate, considering that she was engaged in warfare.

In times of great crisis, we may be so stressed that the appearance of a supernatural being would exacerbate our dilemma rather than alleviate it. Thus, angels appear to us as "real" human beings—the mysterious stranger, who appears suddenly and vanishes just as abruptly.

K.C. of Chicago had an encounter with an angelic mysterious stranger who communicated an important reminder to her about her lifestyle. K.C. said she has been sensitive to supernatural forces since childhood and has had various experiences with them. Angels often give her guidance through synchronicities and through other people. The incident with the mysterious stranger occurred after she had spent a weekend concentrating on "matters unseen and unlimited."

"I was driving back home, a sixteen-hour drive with visits to friends along the way," K.C. said. "It was a brilliant day and I stopped at a restaurant for a sandwich. As I was paying my bill, I saw behind the counter, on the wall, a larger-than-lifesize relief of a figure of a sort of happy-go-lucky bum. It was part of this particular restaurant's theme, meaning the vagabond life on the road. This stylized bum had large, black, bulbous-tipped shoes with a big hole in the toe. As I was paying, I was thinking about how romanticized the 'life of a bum' was depicted, and the chances were than no 'real' bum would be eating in a place like that, as it would be too expensive.

"Well, I was on the road thinking about the weekend intensive, enjoying the brilliant day, thinking about the bum that was depicted on the wall. Later, I stopped to get something to eat at a fast-food burger place, a quick stop off the interstate. When I ordered, I was the only person there, except for a *bum* who came in and stood next to me and placed an order. One thing that caught my attention was that he was very softspoken and was grinning the whole time. He was not disheveled, just wasn't the year's fashion pick.

"He asked if they had pineapple juice. No? Well, they should. And did they have yogurt? No? They should. The young woman behind the counter was amused and slightly bewildered. I thought this guy must come in often, as she seemed to be handling the situation very well.

"He finally ordered something and pulled out a crisp twenty-dollar bill! It was very curious. But the one thing that stopped me cold in my tracks was, when I glanced down at his shoes, I saw the very shoe, with the hole in the toe, that I had seen in the earlier restaurant.

"The significance of what he tried to order first was this: at the time, I was going through some medical changes, and I know from dietary readings and research and my own experience that the acid-alkaline balance is very important to our body's system. Pineapple juice and yogurt would help set that balance up. And this 'bum' standing there ordering reminded me of my own health system concerning the acid-alkaline balance, and how yogurt and juice, so to speak, saved my life once.

"Now, was this an angel? There were no wings. I know it wasn't a hallucination. He didn't talk to me directly, face to face, but I heard everything he said. I left and couldn't find him. I wanted to talk to him. Yet, at the same time I felt I got the message, and I felt a little strange, as I was by myself. I also could have asked the girl behind the counter a question or two, but didn't. Since then, I went to that first restaurant when I was in the area. They have changed their decor. What a shame, I thought.

"I have always felt a strong sense of guidance and protection in my life. I still have an old, slightly crumbling picture with a large gilt frame, that hung over my bed during my youth, of a small boy and girl near a cliff with a large, kind, blue-and-white guardian angel gently guiding them away from danger. To me, these experiences and others have always represented spirits and guidance—angels, if you will. As I have matured, I have come to an understanding of them as not an outer force impinging some bizarre manifestation on me, but rather a response to some powerful *need* I have *in* me."

Angels also can masquerade as legendary figures and spirits of the dead. Perhaps we would resist communication with a supernatural being—especially if we are not certain such a being really exists—but we would be open to communication with a departed loved one. That, then, is how angels would appear to us. In other words, the angelic force will find whatever medium is necessary to connect with us.

Take the case of Steve (a pseudonym), who lives in southern California. When he faced potentially serious health problems, angels came to him in an unexpected way:

"Several years ago, I drove my car to a doctor's office to review laboratory test results drawn from my blood," Steve related. "This was a very serious condition, and as I sat in the parking lot, my body felt heavy and slightly dull from fear and tension. I did not look forward to the ten-minute walk from the parking lot to the doctor's office, where we would review the test results together.

"While still seated in the car, I suddenly became aware of the presence of little children. They were all around me in the interior of the car. While I did not 'see' these children (aged five to twelve years) in the conventional sense through my eyes, I was aware of their various shapes, sizes, and faces through an intuitive faculty or inner eye. As one might imagine, I immediately delighted in their presence and my spirits were uplifted.

"We all got out of the car together and began walking toward the elevators in the attached office building where the doctor's office was. Two little girls walked by my side and held my hands, and perhaps another eight or ten were holding onto my arms, in a sense collectively supporting me as we walked. There was a sense of mirth and laughter, and I was consciously aware of the presence of these blessed creatures, though I am sure they were invisible to the eyes of others who may have been in that same physical space at the time.

"They let me know they were the orphaned children of God and that they were here to cheer me and support me. Knowing that I would soon arrive at the doctor's office, I fought back the urge to cry in joy and relief and settled instead for the blissful, teary-eyed gratitude of their presence.

"As we entered the doctor's office, we all walked up to the receptionist's window to check me in for the appointment. They were still with me, though we all knew we would keep our little secret from others. These divine creatures remained with me. Even now I think fondly of the children and immediately connect with their omnipresent energy.

"As this was about three years ago, it is clear to me

that the divine will desired that I remain in physical form and in good functional health. As in all matters, I say to our beloved Creator, 'Thy will be done.'"

Clearly, our concepts of angels are influenced by thousands of years of historical description and comment, which have imbued certain images into our collective psyche. Yet, as the modern experiences show, angels mutate to fit modern ideas, environments, and situations.

Ultimately, if we become receptive to the presence of the angelic force, and its ability and availability to interact in our lives, then less and less stage clothing will be necessary. Perhaps the ideal image of an angel is none at all but a presence with which we commune via an inner knowing or awareness.

4

Guardian Angels

A popular and certainly appealing type of angel is the guardian angel. The idea of a wise spirit looking out for our welfare is a comforting one. Many cultures believe in a class of spirits the Romans called *manes,* or guardian spirits that have developed from the souls of the dead. The orishas of the Candomblé religion are elementals, or nature spirits, who are assigned in male-female pairs to act as guardian angels. In Spiritualism, and to students of today's New Age, guardian angels are also known as spirit guides. As mentioned in chapter 2, the Greeks believed in daimones, nonhuman intermediary spirits who were either benevolent or malevolent in intent.

Philosopher Rudolf Steiner (1861–1925) said that every person has one guardian angel who has a complete overview of that person's present and previous lives. This view of the big picture gives the angel knowledge of what experiences are necessary in the person's destiny, and it guides the person accordingly. It is limited in its ability to help, however, by its charge's belief in the angel. If the person even recognizes the existence of the angel, then the wheels of celestial guidance are greased.

The Gnostics' guardian angel took the form of the "twin angel." All people, according to this belief, have an enlightened spirit attached to them—their celestial twin. Some Gnostics believed that only very advanced people could communicate with their angels during their lives. Most had to wait until death to be united. However, the Gnostic prophet Valentinus proposed that anyone could contact a twin angel through a rite known as the "bride chamber." In this mystery rite, the human twin is the bride, the angel twin is the groom, and the wedding is the journey of human consciousness into the astral plane.

Helping a human gain access to the astral plane is another function of the guardian angel. If believing will make it so, trying too hard may thwart it. Well-intentioned attempts to connect to dimensions other than our own space-time reality may be stifled by insecurities about our own abilities. The task seems too great. But by believing that we have eager guides who are able to accomplish this task effortlessly, we can turn the task over to them let them make the connection.

There is no dogma in Christianity attesting to guardian angels, though passages in the Bible support the idea. In Exodus, Moses is sent an angel to guard him. Psalms 91:11-13 tells us: "He will give his angels charge of you to guard you in all your ways. On their hands they will bear you up, lest you dash your foot against a stone. You will tread on the lion and the adder, the young lion and the serpent you will trample under foot."

In the apocryphal Book of Tobit, the archangel Raphael, in the guise of a mortal man, accompanies young Tobias on a journey, advises him, guides him, and teaches him magical and healing arts (see chapter 9).

Among the various Christian denominations, belief in guardian angels is strongest in Catholicism. Several movements are devoted to the cult of the guardian angel. Like saints and the Virgin Mary—who also have cults within the Catholic church—guardian angels offer an important means to bring human beings closer to God. Saint Bernard said that it is our duty to love, respect, and trust our guardian angels, and this has become part of the Catholic liturgy.

Angels are not mentioned directly in the Creed in the Mass, which proclaims belief in "one God, the Almighty maker of heaven and earth, of all that is, seen and unseen." The Council of Trent declared that "heaven and earth" encompassed everything contained in heaven and earth, including the angels.

How many guardian angels does a person really have? One, according to the Catholic church, although people with important positions in government are given two: one for them, one for their position. However, one of the early fathers of the Christian church, Origen, wrote that each person has two guardian angels, a good one and a bad one. Like the Greek daimones, the good angels attempt to steer us in the right direction, and the bad angels try to lead us astray. Many people today believe in a single guardian angel—a good angel—though some people feel they have two or more about them.

Just how influential is a guardian angel? The answer is, as influential as we allow them to be. The more we believe in them and call on them, the greater their presence—and influence—in our lives. Saint Thomas Aquinas said angels are able to intervene in our lives because they possess a vastly superior knowledge of the natural universe, as well as a mysterious power over the material world. Thus, what they are capable of doing seems miraculous to us. In addition, they can act on our senses, inspire us and strengthen our minds, causing us to see our situations more clearly, Aquinas said. Merely coming into contact with angels makes us better people. In effect, believing in them liberates our higher selves and our greater creative potential.

Not surprisingly, it has been the leaders of the Catholic church who have kept the flame of faith for the guardian angel in the face of mounting disbelief and skepticism (at least until recently) on the part of the general public, as well as others in the ecclesiastical world.

Pope Pius XI (1857–1939) was on particularly good terms with his guardian angel, praying to him every morning and evening—and in between, if a day was rough. Pius XI did not hesitate to acknowledge this publicly, and even recommended the same to others. He confided to the man who someday would be pope himself, Monsignor Angelo Roncalli (John XXIII, 1881–1963), that angels helped him in his many delicate diplomatic dealings. Prior to a meeting with someone Pius XI needed to persuade, he would pray to his guardian angel, recommending his argument, and asking him to take it up with the guardian angel of the other person. Sometimes Pius XI would himself invoke the guardian angel of the other person, asking to be enlightened as to the other's viewpoint.

Pius XI's experiences influenced John XXIII, who also maintained a deep and abiding faith in guardian angels. He used his radio addresses to exhort followers never to neglect devotion to their guardian angels, who stood ready at all times to help. He particularly urged parents to educate their children that they were not alone but always in the company of their guardian angels. And, like Pius XI, John XXIII sought the help of the guardian angels of those with whom he had difficulties. Even if no difficulties were present, John XXIII always at least acknowledged and paid respect to all guardian angels present at any meeting or gathering. He often acknowledged to his secretary how his guardian angel had inspired him to do various things and had even given him the idea to call an ecumenical council.

Pius XII (1876–1958) did not confide his own personal dealings with angels but did publicly support belief in angels. In an encyclical in 1950, he opined that it was a mistake to question whether angels are "real beings" and that this error in thinking could undermine church doctrine. He urged people to renew their devotion to angels. In 1958, a few days before his death, he gave an address to a group of American tourists, in which he reminded them of the existence of an invisible world populated with angels:

Everyone, no matter how humble he may be, has angels to watch over him. They are heavenly, pure and splendid, and yet they have been given to us to keep us company on our way: they have been given the task of keeping careful watch over you so that you do not become separated from Christ, their Lord.

And not only do they want to protect you from the dangers which waylay you throughout their journey: they are actually by your side, helping your souls as you strive to go ever higher in your union with God through Christ. . . .

We do not want to take leave of you . . . without exhorting you to awaken, to revive your sense of the invisible world which is all around us . . . and to have a certain familiarity with the angels, who are forever solicitous for your salvation and your sanctification. If God wishes, you will spend a happy eternity with the angels: get to know them here, from now on.

In 1968, Pope Paul VI (1897–1978) sanctioned the Opus Sanctorum Angelorum ("the work of the holy angels"), a movement intended to renew and bolster belief in guardian angels and to foster a collaboration between angels and humans for the glory of God, the salvation of humanity, and the regeneration of all creation. There are three phases in the Opus.

In the first phase, initiates make a promise to God that they will love their guardian angels and will respond to their instructions when heard through the voice of conscience. This phase lasts for one year.

In the second phase, the initiates participate in a candlelight ceremony in the presence of the blessed sacrament, in which they consecrate themselves to their "holy guardians." They pledge to become like angels, and to venerate angels, who have been given to humanity by God "in a very special way in these days of spiritual combat for the Kingdom of God."

In the third phase, the initiate participates in a ceremony of consecration to all the angel kingdom.

What the Opus accomplishes is the bringing to life of powerful psychic forces in the individual. Philosopher Michael Grosso observes that believing in the virtually unlimited powers of the guardian angel is a way to release our own "extraordinary potentials."

Many people wonder why, if guardian angels are supposed to protect us as Scripture says, bad things happen in life. Why is one person saved from a tragic accident by the intervention of an angel, and another person is not?

I don't believe that tragedies and difficulties happen because angels desert us. Angels are always with us. For reasons of spiritual and karmic growth, which we may not always be able to fully comprehend, we must at times in our lives go through pain. Some of us do seem to get more than our fair measure of pain, while others of us seem to glide through life beset by few difficulties. Perhaps these circumstances are determined at a very high level of consciousness prior to our coming into the world. However, whenever we are confronted with problems, angels are ready to help us cope. Pain provides us with opportunities for tremendous spiritual growth. Angels are not empowered to make decisions for us about our life's plan. They can only intervene whenever necessary to help keep that plan on track. They also can provide a source of spiritual nourishment when we most need it.

A Healer's Angels

Rosemary Gardner Loveday is one of England's most talented clairvoyants, mediums, and psychic healers. (Her work is discussed in detail in chapter 9.) She is aware of angelic presences as she does her work. Raised and schooled by French Catholic nuns from age five to eleven, Rosemary has always believed in guardian angels. She has always believed she is accompanied by her own guardian angel, whose presence she often feels beside her, especially at night when she says her prayers. Her guardian angel makes himself known, along with other angels.

"They gather around me when I do meditation or say my prayers," Rosemary said. "Thoughts come to me, and I write them down on paper. Once when I was saying my prayers, a voice said to me, 'I'll send a ring of angels to guard you.' Quite plainly! And that's what I feel—that they gather around in a ring."

Rosemary explained that she distinguishes between guardian angels, other angels, and spirits of the dead, who can take on angelic roles. "Everyone has a guardian angel assigned to them, for protection and guidance of our souls, and to help make decisions in life. These angels are assigned to come over here and do that kind of work. We're not always aware of our guardian angels. Some people with more developed intuition are more aware than others."

Rosemary said that one must have faith in the guidance provided by God through guardian angels. "Faith, in a way, is not knowing what's ahead, and handing over your life to God. You may be asked to do some difficult things, perhaps something you think you can't cope with. But if you have faith, you know that God will look after you, and you will always be protected, whatever the circumstances. God is first and foremost the biggest source of love, and he sends angels out to help people. Your guardian angel is always there, and you'll always be protected. So don't be frightened, whatever situation you are sent into."

When Rosemary gives a healing, she often feels other angels, who are not guardian angels, come to assist. These angels seem to come and go, as though they have specific tasks or missions.

In clairvoyant readings, she often senses the presence of souls of the dead, such as relatives of the client. Clients may consider a deceased family member a guardian angel who watches over them, but Rosemary says there is a striking difference between these departed souls and angels. Souls of the dead can be caring and protective, but they do not belong to the same realm as angels—at least not yet.

"I think angels are human souls who have evolved and evolved, probably through lots of lifetimes, to get to the stage of being an angel," Rosemary said. "They work on very high vibrations. I think we come into this world to learn our lessons, such as, we've got to learn patience and learn not to be angry. We've got to develop spiritual qualities. Well, the agony of life is the learning, but if you can grow spiritually, then you become closer to God—and nearer to the angels. I think angels are souls who have gone through the agonies of learning, and they have reached that high level of vibration in realms of light. Then they come back as angels, to bring that light and God's love to people."

Name That Angel

According to the Bible, there are myriads and myriads of angels, yet only two are named: Michael and Gabriel. With so many anonymous angels floating about, is it necessary to find names for them? When we come into awareness of our own guardian angels, do we have to call them by a name? The early Hebrews believed in a complex hierarchy of angels, all with their own names. In mystical Judaism, names have great significance, and manifest various powers.

Yes, we must discover names for our guardian angels if we wish them to manifest in their fullest magnitude. Naming is an important ritual: it defines, and it invests life, power, and potential. Without names, we cannot call out to the higher planes; we cannot invoke or evoke the beings, forces, and energies into our own dimension.

Every mystical, spiritual, magical, or fraternal order the world over has an initiation ritual in which the initiate takes on a new name, usually secret, as a personification of his or her rebirth into the order. The name signifies new powers, new knowledge, a higher spiritual attainment.

William G. Gray, author of some of the most respected contemporary works on the Western mystery tradition, states in *Inner Traditions of Magic* (1970):

The purpose behind the principle of naming anyone or anything at all, is to direct and hold the energy of Consciousness in some particular way at some especial point or portion of Existence. It is essentially an act of concreation, and therefore Magical. Humanity gives names to whatever exists, while Divinity gives Existence to whatever is Named. When a human being "utters a name," the object of that name has its primary existence only in their own mind or "imagination." When Divinity Utters a Name, Existence manifests wherever it is intended, even in material form, because everything including ourselves *is* "in the imagination of God." And *that* is far beyond the imagination of Man.

Thus, discovering one's guardian angel can be likened to an initiation into an order. When we name them, a gateway opens to higher levels of consciousness, and the angel's name is the password. It gives us access and provides us safety as we navigate these higher realms. Naming the guardian angel is one of the most important parts of the Opus Sanctorum Angelorum.

Perhaps the best way to discover the name of a guardian angel is to ask for it in prayer or meditation. The name will arise spontaneously in your thoughts.

Jane M. Howard, of Upperco, Maryland, an author and channeler of angels—and creator of Be an Angel Day—feels it is important to name one's guardian angel. When she gives angel workshops, she tells participants that "the greatest gift you can give to God and the angels is that you believe. By giving an angel a name, you make an offering to God that yes, you believe. You believe in God's kingdom, and you believe in the wonderful being you are going to name. The name creates a rapport between you and your angel, and makes it easier for you to communicate. Angels are going to do their work no matter what we call them. They themselves don't bother with names. But, there will always be a message in the angel's name that comes to you, perhaps relating to your own gifts." Janie describes techniques for naming and communicating with angels in her book *Commune with the Angels*.

Discovering LNO

Alma Daniel, a healing practitioner and psychotherapist in New York City, has been in close contact with her guardian angel, as well as other angels, since the mid-1980s. Their involvement in her life has profoundly influenced her own spiritual growth, her outlook on life, her ability to handle difficulties, and her own work helping others.

Alma is a third-degree Reiki healer and runs a meditation group. In addition, she created Inner Voyages, an empowerment program, and for years ran the Flotation Tank Association and Human Potential Counseling. She is coauthor, with Timothy Wyllie and Andrew Ramer, of *Ask Your Angels*, a handbook for tuning in to the angelic presence via meditation, dreams, and visualizations.

In an interview at her New York City apartment, Alma shared her angel experiences and insights. I was greeted by a lovely atmosphere of serenity and peace, the accumulation of working with the beautiful energies of angels.

"For most of my life, I didn't believe in angels," Alma began. "I thought they existed somewhere, but I didn't really feel there was an angel for me. That was for other people. I think many people feel that way, that maybe there are angels, but they don't have one themselves.

"So, for years I was more in the mind and not so much in the spirit. Then I began studying a variety of teachers and healers, and understood that there was more than just this life and just this person, that there were other forces. But I didn't come into contact with angels until I was in a relationship with a man, Timothy Wyllie, who was very, very dear to me. He was a firm believer in angels, and he kept saying, 'I know you've got an angel, in fact I can sense your angel's presence.' I kept saying that I didn't feel it and didn't believe it.

"Then, in 1985, I got sick with the flu. A lot of trouble had gone down in my life, and sometimes when you have a lot of trouble, you get sick because you just need time to reflect. I was in bed and was looking through some old notebooks that I had kept of various workshops and training that I'd attended to raise my consciousness. I ran across a record of a training I'd done seven years earlier, in which I was asked to visualize a lovely space, to wait for the arrival of my spirit guides and to welcome them when they came. According to my notes, I got two guides. One was a guy in purple tights and an Elizabethan doublet. His name was Greg. I remember thinking at the time, gosh, he's not my type at all. The other was a woman who looked like she was from the 1940s. She had a pompadour hairdo, and her hair was in a snood, and she was wearing a broad-shouldered checked suit. She said her name was Eleanor. I thought, 'Eleanor, that reminds me of my mother, and this couldn't be my guide.' I forgot about the whole experience.

"Timothy came into the room to bring me a cup of tea. He said, 'Your angel is right here now. I can feel her presence. Just ask for her name.''

"I said, 'If you're so smart, *you* ask for her name.' He closed his eyes, and within a moment, he said, 'Elena.' I said, 'No.' I told him the story about the workshop and how Eleanor had come in. I thought it was a common name, and I wasn't going to deal with a common name like that, and Elena sounded just like Eleanor with his English accent.

"Timothy said, 'Okay, you do it. *You* get your angel's name.'

"I said, 'I can't!' He said, "All you do is shut your eyes and ask.'

"So I slammed my eyes shut and asked for the name of my angel. On the back of my forehead, I saw the letters L-N-O: Eleno. Chills went through my body, because I realized that she had tried to come in to me seven years earlier, and I heard the name Eleanor. And Timothy got the name Elena. And when I asked, it wasn't a name as we would call a name, but it was letters, L-N-O. I was totally convinced! Timothy told me to ask her questions, and I started writing down what she was saying. It was something I really didn't want to hear, so I knew that I wasn't making it up.

"From that point on, I've made regular contact with LNO. I do that just by closing my eyes and calling to her, and asking her a question. She will come in and I will write down the answer. Basically, it's channeling.

"Several months later, Timothy and I decided that we needed to put this information out in the world and show other people how to reach their own angels. We started a workshop called Opening to the Angels in December 1985. We asked the angels to bring in exactly the people who needed to be there, and thirty people showed up. We were not sure what we were going to do, but we opened ourselves to guidance, Timothy to his angels and I to my own, and we developed the GRACE process that later we followed."

"What is the process?" I asked.

"GRACE involves basic steps of Grounding, Releasing, Aligning, Conversing, and Enjoying," explained Alma. "You center yourself, feel yourself present, release whatever negativity, doubt, fear, or disappointment that you might have. We were given ways to attune to the angels, ways that people could tune their vibration up to establish a higher frequency so that they would be prepared to speak and to listen to the angels. This work involves the higher chakras: the throat, the heart, the third eye, and the crown. The angels guided us as we went along. We developed meditations in which we would take turns speaking. We never knew what was going to be said in advance, we just trusted." [Chakras are, in Eastern mysticism, energy centers that funnel the universal life force to the body. There are seven major chakras, each associated with a point in the body. The higher ones are more complex than the lower ones, and are involved in psychic and spiritual functions.]

Alma said that she envisions LNO as female, though she doesn't believe that angels have genders. They have both male and female qualities, and present a dominant side to the person. She channels LNO in meditation as well as at her computer. She always records what LNO tells her. Quite often, LNO breaks in when Alma is mildly distracted, such as when she is walking on the street or engaged in some activity.

"About a year after my angel came in I was about to do a very large conference here in New York for float tanks," Alma said. "It was an enormous amount of work, and I was quite concerned about carrying all of it. As I was just walking along the street one day, LNO came in and said, 'Help will be given to you. Don't worry.' I trusted that, and I dropped the agitation I had about whether I was going to be able to pull the conference off. Sure enough, people began appearing to help out with various things. It was a great success—a hundred people showed up from all over the world for this conference."

Alma said that LNO often tells her things she would rather not hear. "I was in the middle of dissolving a relationship that I had been in. It was very painful, and I was at the stage of blame, making wrong, and feeling very disappointed. One day I was walking along the street, going to my exercise class, and LNO's voice came in and said, 'Nobody is doing anything to you. People just do what they do. It's the way you're taking it.' I thought, *Thanks a lot!* But it sparked in me the understanding that I was playing victim and I didn't need to.

"Sometimes people ask me to channel for them. I don't like to do that. I should say, LNO doesn't like to do that, because she feels people have the ability to do that themselves, and it's not good for them to rely on others. It's better for them to go within and to develop that capacity for themselves. Anybody can, you know, it's not given to the few or the chosen. It's an ability that we all have, to hear higher voices, to hear spirit, and to bring that into our lives.

"LNO is a voice, and she often refers to herself as 'we,' not as 'I.' She has told me that she's a voice in a collective of angels whose function is to connect people with their higher selves. That's specifically her function, to oversight everything that I do, so that if I bring her in, it's my higher self that is operating at that point. Then I'm not coming from little self or little me. I'm coming from the higher view, which is much more expansive."

"Do you hear LNO as an inner voice or an external voice?" I asked.

"Her voice is within me. There is a school of thought that says that angels are actually aspects of our higher selves. That's not a foreign concept to me. In other words, it could very well be that I've had to externalize part of myself and see it as coming from other than myself in order to give it the credence and the respect that I do. Maybe I wasn't prepared to give myself that, but I could give that to my higher self in the form of an angel."

"Do you experience other angels besides LNO?"

Alma nodded. "Sometimes other angelic presences come in for me as a feeling. The emotion is always a heart-opening, expanding love and tenderness and compassion. It is so palpably felt, Rosemary, the tears will come to my eyes and roll out of my eyes. I'm not sobbing, it's joyful. It's being in a place of such utter acceptance and love and compassion that you know you're home.

"I don't see angels," she continued. "Other people are blessed in that kind of vision. I feel angels emotionally. I can feel it almost as a texture of changes in the air—it's a particular quality. Sometimes it's like silk, sometimes it's like velvet. But obviously these are other senses that I'm using. They're not my physical senses."

"What have your experiences led you to believe about the nature of angels?" I asked.

"The angel is a manifestation of God force. Just as we are a different manifestation of God force. Much of the time, we're not acting in a godly way, but we have that capability within us. So, the angel is a reminder of who we really are, of a god within, of the divinity within us. The angel is also a particular source of comfort and reassurance. As people reach out to their angels, they begin to bring them more into the mainstream of their lives. The angel inspirits them. Now, the question is, are they being inspirited by the angel or are they just connecting to their own God spirit? I don't know, and I don't think it matters, because the outcome is the same—human beings learning to be more human and more humane, not only to others, but to ourselves as well. It always seems easier to be good to other people than it is to be good to ourselves. When you really begin to dance with the angels and to live with the angels and to work, eat, and sleep with the angels, you take on a more loving way with yourself. Then your contact with other people is vastly improved. Angels remind us about caring, about showing tenderness, and about showing respect."

"How can someone tell when they've contacted an angel? Is there a distinct feature to the voice or feelings involved?"

Alma said, "I've done a lot of work teaching people how to channel or contact their angels, and I'm always looking out for what's not an angel. The angel is never going to tell you, *'You done wrong! You bad!'* The angel will approach whatever calamity or catastrophe you have created with a higher view, and will point out that you've chosen this or brought this into your life for the purpose of evolving and growing more in the light. If you get a transmission and it scolds you or criticizes you or tells you what to do, such as 'Move to

Florida now,' don't trust that. It's not coming from your angel.

"I do make a distinction between angels and spirit guides. The spirit guide is generally a spirit that has been in physical form. Angels have never been incarnated in physical form. They've always been angels. Spirit guides can seem like angels to some people. However, they're concerned with the day-to-day life, while angels are much more concerned with uplifting your life to embrace the celestial—a knowing of greater realms, where values are quite different. The guides seem to have values which are of a very mundane level."

"Why is it so important for people to be more open to angels?"

"We're at a turning point of evolution, which, in terms of consciousness, is probably as great as the point in evolution when man first starting using his opposable thumb, discovered fire, and began to be a more conscious being," said Alma. "We're moving into a higher level of consciousness now, which is God consciousness. You're familiar with the idea that the second coming of Christ will be as a woman?"

I nodded.

"What that really means is that the feminine Christ consciousness is coming down now, into each one of us. It is the feminine principle that is being returned to the earth. The feminine principle represents the nurturer, the guardian, and the caretaker. We need a return of this energy because we've been dominated by a patriarchy. As we move into this consciousness of the feminine Christ, we are beginning to develop and embody the feminine qualities of compassion, caring, forgiveness, and universal, unconditional love.

"We've had to be pushed to the very edge to get here. We've had to desecrate our home, Mother Earth. We've had to pillage and abuse our brothers and sisters. The atrocities are incredible. We've got to know that it's within each one of us to be the bearers of light. That's why we need to connect with angels."

Alma said that being in touch with her guardian angel makes difficulties in life easier to bear and overcome. "Since the angel has come into my life, no matter what happens to me, I welcome it as a part of my growth, even though I might not like it. I know that if I embrace every experience, I will grow. My angel tells me that you will never finish your growth. She said that even after you leave the physical plane, you continue to evolve, though in a different way."

Be An Angel Day

Our guardian angels may look after us on the mundane level, but one of their most important tasks is to help us grow spiritually, and that means inspiring us to be like angels to other people. Toward that end, the angels inspired Janie Howard, whom I mentioned earlier in this chapter, to create Be An Angel Day. The angel holiday was launched on August 22, 1993.

Janie is a woman of great talent who uses her gifts to help others, especially to help them develop their own ways of connecting to the angelic kingdom. She lives and works in the same area where she grew up, the rolling green countryside of Maryland. She founded a nonprofit charitable organization, Angel Heights, dedicated to spreading the work of angels. Janie has been communing with angels since she was a teen. About a decade ago, she met a medium who informed her that she herself would soon begin to work as a medium. Janie's gift opened up and, with training and practice, she is now an open channel, which means she receives information from her angelic host all the time.

She clairvoyantly sees angels as ripples and waves of light around other people, and also has seen angels that have taken on human form. Angels, she says, "represent God. Angels can be everything and anything in order to inspire you, and to guide you and touch you."

The purpose of Be An Angel Day is service to others. The motto is 'Be an Angel, do one small act of service for someone, be a blessing in someone's life.' By doing this, said Jane, we take on angelic energy ourselves.

The angels chose August because it is the eighth month of the year, which in numerology is the number of achievement, accomplishment, and fulfillment, and is a master vibration number, the number of the master architect of all. Be An Angel Day is a project on a master level, the building of a bridge between two kingdoms.

The angels also directed Janie to have as the "official sponsor" of Be An Angel Day something called The Angel Alliance, which really exists in spirit. The angels specifically did not want the day associated with any one person or organization.

Ultimately, every day should be Be An Angel Day.

5

How Angels Come Among Us

Direct Intervention

Benvenuto Cellini (1500–1571), an Italian goldsmith, sculptor, and author, tells in his autobiography, *The Life of Benvenuto Cellini* (published posthumously in 1728) how an angel saved his life in prison. Cellini, a hotheaded man, was constantly engaging in scrapes and fights with other people. On several occasions he was imprisoned and was condemned to death. He was absolved once for murder, by Pope Paul III.

In 1535, he was jailed in Rome on charges of stealing the jewels of Pope Clement. Cellini was incarcerated high in the towers of the Castel Sant'Angelo. He made a daring attempt to escape by scaling down the castle walls on a rope made of bedsheets tied together. He was captured and thrown into the dungeon. While in the dungeon, he sank into despair and resolved to kill himself by hanging. Just as he was about to hang himself, a tremendous invisible force knocked him back. An angelic youth appeared to him in a vision and lectured him about the importance of living. Cellini was released from the dungeon on the personal request of a cardinal. He went on to become one of the most celebrated artists of the Renaissance.

We've seen some other examples of how angels intervene directly in our lives, such as the invisible force that knocked Robert S. off the live wire, saving his life, and the pillar of light that appeared to Juliet Hollister.

Angels also intervene directly in the form of human beings. Typically, these are "mysterious strangers" who appear suddenly in times of distress. They know just what to do to solve someone's plight. Once the rescue has been made, they suddenly vanish. No one ever knows who they are.

Mysterious strangers can be male or female. Most often they are male—usually a fresh-looking, clean-cut youth. They are invariably well-dressed, polite, and knowledgeable about the crisis at hand. They speak, though they talk sparingly, and they will even take hold of the people in distress.

One need not be in dire straits to have a mysterious stranger angel appear on the scene, as the following story from Linda Auer of La Grange, Illinois, illustrates:

"I went into a local electronics store with my son, who had his newly purchased shortwave radio. He had been having difficulty receiving certain channels and believed there was a problem with the radio. We began a discussion with the store manager. My son began to explain the problem, but the manager cut him off, trying to make it sound like my son didn't know how to operate the radio. The more my son tried to object, the more insistent the manager became.

"Suddenly, out of nowhere, this young man appeared at the register where we were standing, and intervened. He had something in his hand to purchase and said very quietly, yet with knowledge, that my son had a point. He proceeded to explain very calmly to the manager what the problem was. Not only did he solve the problem, but suddenly the manager was much nicer. Then the man purchased the item in his hand. It was *crystals* for a shortwave.

"I was just dumbfounded. The young man wished us a nice day and left the store. A couple of seconds later, I rushed out the door to thank him, but he was *gone*. He literally disappeared. The store is in the middle of the block, so you would still be able to see someone walking down the sidewalk. Obviously, this was not an ordinary human. I still get chills when I think about it."

The angelic "roadside rescue" happens so often that it is almost a cliché in angel lore. In the roadside rescue, the mysterious stranger arrives to help the motorist stranded on a lonely road at night or injured in an accident in an isolated spot. Or, human beings arrive just in the nick of time.

Jane Howard is on the road around the world a great deal to lecture and give workshops. The angels have come to her aid a number of times, helping her avert accidents by instructing her what to do or taking invisible control of the wheel or pedals. One night the gas pedal in Janie's car became stuck, and she ran off the freeway near Baltimore. She stopped the car by throwing the transmission into park. It would not restart, and she began to panic. It was 10 P.M. and she was miles from the nearest exit. She prayed to the angels for help, and within minutes a van pulled up, carrying a man and a woman. The woman rolled down her window and told Janie not to be frightened, for they were Christians. Even so, many people would have been wary of strangers at night. But the angels gave Janie assurances, and she accepted a ride to a gas station. She discovered that the couple lived in a town near hers, and knew her family. They pulled off to help Janie, they said, because they had a daughter, and they hoped that if their daughter ever was in distress, she, too, would be aided.

Prayer and Meditation

Prayer is a powerful way to commune with the divine. Prayer directs psychic energy toward accomplishment. The noted healer Ambrose Worrall (1899–1972), who practiced faith healing in Baltimore with his famous wife, healer Olga Worrall (1906–1985), once said that all thoughts are prayers. Thus, we should constantly strive to tune our thoughts to the highest expressions possible of love, benevolence, and goodwill.

Angels listen to our thoughts and prayers. If you pray for their guidance and are sincere and receptive, the guidance will be given.

Carol Ann Durepos, a graphoanalyst in Clovis, New Mexico, told me about a prayer experience she had that evoked a churchful of angels. It occurred in July 1978, during a time when she was coping with family problems and the death of a friend. She went to evening mass to pray but was so tired that she couldn't seem to settle into her usual prayer, which is the mantra of "Jesus."

"My concentration just wasn't there, so I started to say my mantra out loud," Carol said. "I was feeling down, not necessarily depressed, but world-weary. It seemed I couldn't do anything right at the time. I felt an urge to open Scripture. I had my little Gideon King James Bible with me in my purse, and I cracked it to Acts 4, verse 10. I was overjoyed when I read it [it mentions the name of Jesus as healer]. I felt approval at my efforts despite my weariness. I felt heard and acknowledged.

"I was able to just settle down and pray when all of a sudden the whole church appeared to be filled up with moving light, flashes, and singing. I felt like the angels, saints, seraphim, and cherubim were all rejoicing with me and that the very universe, even the stones, sings praise when the name of Jesus is said or spoken. Don't ask me how, but I felt like the very name of Jesus is a caress to the Father, like a whisper of a kiss to his cheek. I can't tell you how long it lasted, or whether I saw with my open eyes. It felt like I did see with my eyes—the church was completely full of color, sounds, and movement, like it was going to burst open."

This experience was so powerful that it gave Carol a feeling of sustained guidance that stayed with her through resolving her difficulties. "I felt led all the way," she said.

Carol calls herself "a very ordinary quester." Her experience also has opened her up to many visions and insights, and she teaches others how to meditate.

Alma Daniel, whom we met in the previous chapter, has counseled people internationally on how to reach angels through meditation. "Sit in a quiet and peaceful place," she suggested. "Ground yourself and put your hand on your heart, which connects you to your own loving nature. Close your eyes and imagine the presence of your angel around you. How does that feel? Maybe you feel yourself being enclosed by these wonderful wings. Or maybe you feel yourself growing lighter. Whatever it is, acknowledge what you experience. Just stay with it. Notice how you're feeling, what your breathing is like. It's through the imagination that angels can come to us. If we can conceive of it, it can happen. Then ask the angel for its name. Or ask, 'Please be with me,' or 'Help me in this day.' Angels are here to help—they're not decorative. I ask for help in getting subway trains. I ask for help when I have to do a lot of errands. Now, I don't consider that my own guardian angel, LNO, handles these particular functions, but there are other angels that do so. And don't forget to say thank you!

"I always tell people to write down what they get. You'll know if it's your own thoughts. Quite often, angels tell us something we don't expect to hear, or don't want to hear. Communication also often comes in unbidden. You can't reach the angels willfully. You can only reach them through surrender. You can't command, *Now I will speak with my angel! Now!'* Rather, you have to open yourself as a tool, an instrument for them to come through you. Always be grateful for the blessings in your life—it's a great pathway to angelic contact."

Dreams

We have only to look at the Bible for some of the earliest stories about how angels appear to us in dreams. Genesis relates to us the story of Jacob, son of Isaac and Rebecca, who was hunted by his twin brother, Esau. Jacob escaped to his uncle. En route he had a dream of angels ascending and descending a ladder to heaven. God promised him and his descendants the land on which he slept. "I will not leave you until I have done all that I promised you," God said.

Joseph, husband to Mary, the mother of Jesus, similarly was given important messages by angels in dreams, we are told in the Book of Matthew. While betrothed to Mary, Joseph learned of her pregnancy and resolved to divorce her quietly. Before he did so, an angel appeared to him in a dream and said, "Joseph, son of David, do not fear to take Mary your wife, for that which is conceived in her is of the Holy Spirit; she will bear a son, and you shall call his name Jesus, for he will save his people from their sins."

Joseph followed the angel's instructions. After Jesus was born, Joseph was again contacted by an angel through his dreams. The angel told him to take Mary and Jesus and flee Bethlehem, for King Herod was intent to search for the child and destroy him. Joseph, Mary, and Jesus fled to Egypt, where they remained until Herod was dead.

That angels appear in dreams is significant, for dreams have a reality of their own—they are just as real as our waking consciousness. In dreams we leave the boundaries of the physical world behind and travel to higher, more subtle planes. These planes are more subjective, but the subjectivity does not render dreams any less "real."

This fundamental wisdom about the reality of dreams has been understood since ancient times. The early Greeks and Romans believed that the soul traveled while the body was asleep. The soul would go to otherworldly realms wherein dwelled the lesser spirits who mediated between humans and the gods. Plato called this realm "the between." Here the human soul had experiences and encounters that had the same validity as experiences during waking life. What made the dream experiences more special, however, were their supernatural characteristics. In dreams, it was possible to meet the gods, to see the distant past or future, and to be healed of illness and disease.

The "between state" is where we commune with angels while asleep. They can appear to give us information or inspiration. They may appear as angels, or as mysterious beings, or be disguised as human beings, just as they sometimes are on the physical plane.

Dream literature provides numerous accounts of writers, poets, scientists, musicians, and inventors who were directly inspired by dreams. Many arrived at answers to questions and solutions to problems that had eluded them in waking consciousness. Were they given those inspirations by angels, who used the fertile medium of the dream to plant ideas?

Physicist Niels Bohr saw the model for the atom in a dream, and the nineteenth-century Russian chemist Mendeleyev had a dream vision of the periodic table of elements. Artist William Blake was shown a process for copper engraving in a dream; the inexpensive production technique then enabled him to make a living from his mystical illustrations. Author Robert Louis Stevenson received the idea for *The Strange Case of Dr. Jekyll and Mr. Hyde* in a dream, and poet Samuel Taylor Coleridge wrote his fragment, "Kubla Khan," word for word as he remembered it from a dream. He might have completed his work had he not been interrupted while committing it to paper. When he returned to his task, he discovered, unhappily, that it had evaporated from memory. Dreams are fleeting —they must be recorded immediately on awakening if we are to retain and benefit from their content.

Austin Osman Spare, a brilliant English artist whose work was largely overlooked in his lifetime (1886–1956), received much inspiration in the dream state. He produced psychic art in which he reified elementals, spirits, and primal forces he experienced in the alternate reality of dreams. His dreams were so real to him that often he thought the dreams were the real world and waking life was a dream. "Occasionally I have done work, and have been entirely unconscious of having done it," he said in an interview with *Psychic News* in 1932. "I must have got up from the bed, done the painting, and then returned to bed without wakening. The wealth of ideas that are expressed is amazing. I once executed a hundred drawings in three or four hours."

The ancients believed that such inspirations were indeed gifts from the gods. Or, as we might think today, from angels.

Patricia P., of Harrison, New York, is a born-again Christian who feels in close communion with God,

Jesus, and angels. "I feel I have a lot of angels around me because that's what it says in the Bible—there are many of them around us," she told me. Angels, she said, helped her rescue her little niece from drowning one day. The experience began with a dream.

"One night several years ago, I was in my bed at home in a house with my brother and his wife," Patricia said. "I felt led by the Word—an inner feeling that I believe is Jesus Christ—telling me to pray that there would be angels around the swimming pool outside. We have a small above-ground pool in the backyard. There are a lot of children in the neighborhood, including my niece and nephew, who go into the pool. So, I prayed as directed. I envisioned angels standing around the pool's ledge facing inward. They looked like Roman guards, ready for protection. I don't know why they had that appearance, that's just how they popped up. I didn't anticipate that there might be an accident. In fact, I kind of questioned why I had been directed to pray that.

"A day or two later, I found myself in the pool with the little children. I don't know why I got in—I usually don't use it. Mostly it's for the kids. They splash around with floaters on their arms to keep them up. I was standing in the water at one edge, and a friend came over and started talking to me, diverting my attention.

"My sister was nearby but out of sight. She suddenly felt the Lord say to her, 'Check on Lisa,' her daughter, who is two and a half years old. She looked around and realized Lisa was not present. 'Patty, is Lisa in the pool?' she called out. I didn't hear her, and she called out again, 'Patty, is Lisa in the pool?' I heard her, and turned around just in time to see my little niece step off the ladder into the pool at the other end without her little floaters on. She sank immediately underwater. 'Oh, my God!' I shouted, and I started running toward her in the water. But the water was heavy, and it seemed like I couldn't get to her in time. Then I heard an authoritative masculine voice, about a foot away from my right ear, say, 'Swim to her!' I felt a presence, as though someone were standing near to me.

"I swam to Lisa, and I scooped her out of the water by her arms. Her eyes were open so wide they almost seemed to pop out of her head. By then my sister had reached the pool, and she took Lisa and began banging her on the back. Water spurted out of her mouth, and she coughed and began breathing again. She was all right!

"I thank the Lord that her life was saved. Lisa didn't suffer any damage. Truly, it was a miracle.

"Later, I asked the Lord whose voice I'd heard in the pool, that said, 'Swim to her!' It wasn't the voice of Jesus, because I know that voice. The answer was given to me that it was an angel. And I know it was."

Since then, Patricia said, she has called on angels many times whenever she feels in need of their protection or guidance.

Dreams were the initial medium of my own encounters with an angel I named Silver Lady. In the mid-1980s, I started to have periodic dreams that were significantly different from my dreaming pattern. I usually dream in color, but these dreams were almost always in black and white. The setting was always an alien landscape, unlike anything I'd ever seen on earth. The landscapes often were bleak and barren, sometimes like deserts, sometimes like the moon. Sometimes the setting was nothing but blackness, like the black void of space.

In these dreams, I was always in the company of a tall woman dressed in flowing garments of a luminescent silver—hence my moniker for her, Silver Lady. We never spoke but communicated telepathically. Only once did I see her face. It had no features like a human countenance. Instead, it was a swirl of iridescent color, like mother-of-pearl.

Silver Lady always seemed to be taking me somewhere for the purpose of instruction, though when I awoke, I could never remember exactly what it was that I had been told. I had some ideas from the imageries. For example, I was shown other worlds where realities were unlike that of the earth. I was taken into space and shown how to make a path of light for myself, by projection of thought. It seemed that I was being introduced to the multidimensional nature of consciousness and to the tremendous power of thought. I was getting lessons in how we create our reality with our thought: we can either live in our own fear and darkness or we can light our own way and the way for others.

The dreams with Silver Lady became more frequent. They were wonderful and adventuresome, and I missed them if a period of time went by without one. I assumed her to be an angel.

Then something spectacular happened.

In late 1986, I was commissioned to write *The Encyclopedia of Witches and Witchcraft,* the first of my books dealing with the paranormal and related topics. I mapped out a research plan to follow witch-craft into modern-day practices and beliefs. This brought me into contact with individuals who practice the religion of Witchcraft (or Wicca), various recon-structions of pagan rites that celebrate Goddess. There is a connection here between Silver Lady and Goddess. Goddess is associated with the moon, and the moon is associated with silver; hence, silver is the color and metal of Goddess. Moon and Goddess rule the intuition, the deep unconscious, the forces of nature, and the interconnectedness that binds all things. They rule creativity—the ability to create with thought. And, in Wicca, Goddess is often referred to as The Lady.

I was deep into my research when one night I had a prototypical "encounter." Encounters with nonphysi-cal and nonhuman beings often follow a pattern. They take place in the dead of night. The percipient is often paralyzed. There is telepathic communication that seems to infuse the percipient with information. There may be paranormal phenomena, such as levita-tion or the psychokinetic (mind over matter) move-ment of objects.

I awoke at about 3 A.M. to find Silver Lady standing beside the bed. She looked real and solid, though she glowed with a shimmery silver light. She was holding her arms outstretched, as though she were going to bend down and touch me. But we never made physical contact. Instead, a stream of energy poured through her hands, entering me between and slightly above the brows, where the third eye chakra is located, and in the chest, where the heart chakra resides.

This energy seemed to be a data stream. Bits were

coming into me at a tremendous speed. I felt as though I were being downloaded by a cosmic computer. Information or knowledge was pouring into me so fast that I could not discern what it was. It was all I could do to absorb it, and I didn't feel I could do that without literally exploding. Yet I was powerless to shut it off, for I was paralyzed and held flat to the bed by an invisible force.

The infusion seemed to last forever, though the entire episode probably was over in a matter of moments. At some point, I felt I could no longer absorb it, and the connection was terminated. Silver Lady vanished. I felt disoriented, got up for a few moments, and then returned to bed and fell immediately asleep.

The experience had a profound effect on me. I hadn't been shaken or scared by it, but I wasn't certain what had taken place. My interpretation is that I was infused with a blueprint of my work in this life. Even though years have passed, I still can't say exactly what that blueprint is. I don't think it's for me to know at the level of mundane consciousness. I've been asked to trust in the guidance provided, and I have done so. I believe that the general purpose I chose for this life is to help people on their spiritual quests through my writing and lecturing. The blueprint concerns the specifics for the execution of that purpose.

With the infusion, a major role for Silver Lady was completed. She has not appeared in any dreams, nor has she made any nocturnal appearances. It was years before she made herself noticed again, in a session with the noted English medium and healer Eddie

Burks (see chapter 8). Yet, although she has moved to the background, I feel her guiding presence is with me.

Visions, Apparitions, and Voices

A mystical vision is perhaps the most dramatic way an angel can manifest. Unlike the mysterious stranger, who has the appearance of a flesh-and-blood human being, angels in mystical visions are bathed in a glory of light and radiate supreme joy and love. The percipient is overwhelmed by the light and love, and is in awe of being in proximity to the Deity through his emissaries, the angels. Such visions usually have an instructional purpose and a tremendous transformative effect on the person who experiences them.

Many spiritual leaders have received their initiation by way of an angelic mystical vision. Enoch's visions were described in chapter 2. Various other biblical figures, when they were called by God to be prophets, experienced mystical visions of heaven and angels. For example, Isaiah, who lived in the late eighth century B.C., was shown the throne of God, encircled by seraphim.

Muhammad (c. 571–632), the founder of Islam, received the revelations that became the Koran in a series of angelic visions. In 610, Muhammad was forty years old and living a life of asceticism when, one night in his dreams, the archangel Gabriel appeared and gave him the first revelation of the Koran, the holy book that contains the doctrine of Islam. Muslims call this event the Night of Power. For the rest of his life, Muhammad fell into nearly daily trances, during which he received the remainder of the Koran, which totals 6,666 verses. Sometimes the material was delivered by angels, and sometimes via clairaudient voices. Muhammad's trances were heavy and torporous, and his breath was labored. It was not until three years after his first vision that Muhammad began his new calling as a prophet, preaching first to members of his own clan.

Joseph Smith (1805–1844), the founder of Mormonism (the Church of Jesus Christ of Latter-day Saints), had various visions, including those of angels and pillars of light, which contributed to persecution against him. On the night of September 21, 1823, he was awakened by a brilliant light flooding his room. The light revealed the angel Moroni, a messenger from God. Moroni told Smith that he had helped write, then bury, a history written on gold plates by his father, Mormon, of an ancient people descended from Israel who had lived and died in America. Moroni said that Christ had appeared to these people after his resurrection, and that they had established a church, but that knowledge of the gospel was lost in a great fratricidal war. God had chosen Smith to retrieve the plates, translate them, and reestablish the church in preparation for the latter days prior to the Second Coming.

Moroni appeared to Smith three times during that night, and again the next day. He revealed the hiding place of the gold plates but instructed Smith to wait four years before digging them up. Smith did as ordered and retrieved the plates on September 22, 1827. He also recovered seer stones, the Urim and Thummim, and their breastplate.

The plates were covered with strange symbols resembling hieroglyphics. They created quite a stir among the public. To avoid harassment, Smith went away to Pennsylvania (he was living in western New York State at the time). He translated the symbols with the help of an itinerant school teacher. The result, the *Book of Mormon,* was published in 1830. Moroni recovered the plates and the stones.

Teresa of Avila (1515–1582), Spanish mystic and Carmelite nun, began experiencing mystical visions and revelations in 1555. She evaluated her visions through several criteria, which can be used today in evaluating encounters with angelic beings:

The visions have a sense of power and authority.

They produce tranquility, recollectedness, and a desire to praise God.

They impart an inner certainty that what is envisioned is true.

They are clear and distinct, with each part carrying great meaning.

They result in a life of improved ethics and increased psychological integration.

Emanuel Swedenborg (1688–1772) traveled often to heaven in his mystical flights. The Swedish scientist and scholar led a fairly routine life until 1743, when he was fifty-six. The spiritual world was thrust upon him one night in a dream, during which he visited the higher planes. For the rest of his life he experienced mystical dreams, visions, and ecstatic trances, in which he communicated with angels (the souls of the dead), Jesus and God, and visited heaven and hell. He was shown the order of the universe, which was significantly different from the teachings of the Christian church. Swedenborg understood that he had been chosen by God to see these things and record them to teach others.

Swedenborg quit his government job and lived on a half pension in order to devote his entire attention to his visions. Initially he had to rely on their spontaneity, but eventually he learned to induce trances through breath control. Some of his trances were so deep that he remained in them for up to three days, seemingly barely alive. While in light trances, he recorded the dictations of angels.

The experiences stimulated a tremendous outpouring of written works, which led to the founding of a religion in his name, the Church of the New Jerusalem.

These are but a few examples of mystical visions involving angels. Few people in modern times have such dramatic experiences. Perhaps one reason is that our society does not foster an environment conducive to visions and prophecies. Consequently, our state of consciousness tends to be closed to these types of openings to other realities.

Some modern angel encounters do involve visual apparitions. The most common forms are columns or pillars of light, or balls of light. No figures or forms are seen in these lights, which usually are a bright (sometimes dazzlingly bright) light of white or silver. The percipient receives mental impressions that these light-forms are angels. Sometimes figures or outlines of figures are perceived within the light. They are invariably human in shape. People occasionally see wings, which typically are as large as the figure itself.

It is not uncommon for the lower portions of the figure to fade off into nothingness, or for hands, feet, and faces to be poorly defined or not defined at all.

Angels also can appear as visions on the inner planes, that is, seen with the inner eye. As such, they are more perceptions—an awareness—than an image that seems external. Clairvoyance and clairaudience (an inner voice) are two ways that some psychically gifted people communicate with a host of spirit beings, and visit other realities. Those who are not psychically gifted are likely to have at least one or several clairvoyant or clairaudient experiences during their lives. Such experiences, especially if they involve angels, are so wonderful that the individual longs for a repeat of them—often to no avail. The experiences happen when we need them, not when we want them.

Rudolf Steiner (1861–1925), founder of Anthroposophy, had numerous experiences on higher planes through clairvoyance and clairaudience, and perhaps out-of-body travel. Anthroposophy is a unique blend of Rosicrucian, Theosophical, and Christian traditions. Through deep and concentrated meditation, Steiner learned to access nonphysical realms, including the Akashic Records, said to be master records of everything that has ever occurred in deed or thought since the beginning of the universe. The Akashic Records exist as impressions on the astral plane. Steiner learned a great deal about angels, which he described in detail in his writings and many lectures.

Like Pseudo-Dionysius, Steiner also saw nine orders of angels in a hierarchy around God. However, he gave the levels different names and descriptions. Steiner believed his own spiritual work to be in the service of the archangel Michael, who, he said, is directing the evolution of the human spirit into the third millennium.

Plato to the Rescue

In addition to dreams and the bedside encounter, I've had clairaudient encounters with angels. At about the same time that Silver Lady was manifesting in my life (the mid-1980s), I became aware of another angelic presence around me: a being who calls himself Plato (yes, angels *do* have a sense of humor!). Plato—not to be confused with the human Plato—is a "speaking angel," whose purpose is to assist me in delivering talks.

Standing up in front of a group and giving a talk is something that has come naturally to me since grade school. I was ten years old when I discovered this gift. In school, we were assigned to develop and give presentations on a subject of our choice to our classmates. I chose astronomy, which was my passionate interest. Most of the other kids gave ten- to fifteen-minute talks. Mine lasted nearly an hour. So caught up was I in the subject and the chance to expound on it, that I machine-gunned my audience with an armchair tour of the universe. My teacher's only criticism of my organization, content, and delivery was that I talked too fast. Later in school, I joined the debate team and won an award in one competition for team debating. So, extemporizing has always been easy. I rarely use notes.

Some years ago, I was invited to speak at a writer's conference in Tacoma, Washington, and deliver a talk on law and the writer. The topic was rather out of my bailiwick, but I was anxious to go, so I accepted. To my dismay, I had a dreadful time preparing the talk, which was supposed to fill two hours. It just wouldn't gel, and every time I tried to run through it, I couldn't get even part way through without suffering a total block. A detailed outline and notes failed to help. Nothing like this had ever happened to me before.

I arrived at the conference petrified that I would stumble my way through the talk, fail to give people what they'd paid to hear, and look like an idiot. The morning I was to speak, I awoke to hear an external voice say into one ear, "You have your material well in hand." The voice was neither male nor female, but it was quite authoritative.

At that point I quit worrying, even though I still didn't have the foggiest idea of what I was going to say. Not only did I quit worrying, but I felt the most remarkable peace and calm come over me. As I began my talk, I felt a distinct shift in my consciousness, as though part of me were displaced to one side. In addition, I could feel the weight of an invisible presence on my shoulders, as though a being perched there, much as a child would straddle an adult's shoulders. I talked for two hours without looking at a single note, and got rave comments from the audience. "You don't know it, but you're a born teacher!" one woman enthused afterward. I could only privately thank the angel who rescued me from a tight spot.

Now, a skeptic would say that the stress of the situation simply unlocked my own knowledge and enabled me to deliver it. I was, after all, an experienced speaker. A skeptic would explain the external voice as my own inner voice. I emphatically do not agree. I believe I was helped by an angel, and that is how I find meaning in this experience. Furthermore, the experience crystallized a source of help to me in all future speaking situations. Since that time, I have not begun a talk without first thanking Plato for his assistance. As time has gone on, I have been increasingly aware of this shift in consciousness when I deliver a talk. Occasionally, someone who is clairvoyant will come up to me afterward and ask me if I know I have an angel or a being standing off to one side of me. "Yes," I say, "that's my speaking angel!"

Channeling

Roseann Cervelli has been channeling angels for about a decade. She works with a small group of people who meet regularly in her home in Martinsville, New Jersey. Like others who have been touched by angels, Roseann has experienced spiritual growth and tremendous changes in her outlook on life and her approach to living. Some of her channelings have been published in a book, *Voices of Love.*

"I was raised Catholic and I've always had a strong sense of spirituality," Roseann told me. "In my twenties, I went through a period of questioning the church, and I became increasingly unsatisfied with the way it dealt with issues and people because of outdated rules and regulations. I went through an agnostic searching. I studied Edgar Cayce's material for a number of years. And I began studying about healing and consciousness, and the Christ consciousness.

"Around 1980, I received a laying on of hands from a priest, who later became my mentor. I experienced a feeling of peace, like an opening. After that, for the next year or so, I studied with the priest and other like-minded people. I would have a kind of mystical experience. I would be pulled into a oneness and meditative state, and it would be so wonderful that I would find myself in tears, just in being one with everybody on the earth. I'd see a face, like the face of my daughter, and then her face became somebody else's face, which became somebody else's face, and so on, and before I knew it, I was enveloped in this oneness. These were my first experiences with the spiritual energies—very loving and very embracing. I didn't understand at all what happening. I thought I was going crazy. But I trusted the experience, because it *was* happening to me."

The mystical experiences lasted for about a year and then subsided. By then Roseann was able to enter meditative states easily on her own. At the end of 1981, she met a woman who channeled an entity named Matthew.

"Matthew spoke to me about healing and about how, if I wanted to be a healer, I had to learn to love myself. He told me to do a meditation each day where I would walk along a beach, and see myself lifted up on a cloud. There I would meet Jesus or a lighted entity and would be taken to a library, where I would just absorb knowledge. I didn't have to know what that knowledge was, but I just had to be there. Then I would come back down to earth and spread that knowledge around.

"I did that meditation for about a week when the writing started. I was in my house vacuuming and being a regular housewife, and all of a sudden I got this energy coming through my head. I heard the words, 'Pick up your pen and write.' It was such a loving energy, and such a driving energy at the same time, so that's what I did. The first words that came out are the first words in my book, *Voices of Love:* 'Words are the essence of God.' The writing lasted maybe five minutes. It was quite an experience, because the thoughts were coming faster than I could write them down. I was hearing them from a different part of my being. They weren't coming just from my head the way I would normally write—the thoughts were almost ahead of themselves. I wrote quickly and my hand was shaking, there was all this energy. Then it stopped as quickly as it started."

Excited, Roseann called her priest mentor, who said, "Praise God, this is a wonderful gift! Sit with it and see what happens."

She did, and a few minutes later, the channeling resumed, again for a few minutes. "I was in wonder at what was unfolding," Roseann said. "After that, I would feel called to write almost at any time—during the middle of the night, two o'clock in the morning. I finally had to ask to receive three times a day, so that it wouldn't disrupt my life.

"What I was given were little essays on spiritual concepts, like forgiveness, belonging, oneness, healing, and the healing touch. They were all teaching me to live a healing life. Anytime I said or did anything, I would be aware of the impact. I also saw how I could use any situation to bless other people and myself as well, because I was tuned in to the Source, and I would be channeling love from the Source. I got to understand about the soul. As I wrote, it transformed me. It was like there was a spirit in my head, and it would go into my heart and I would emotionally *feel* what I was writing, and I could feel it changing me as I wrote."

The beings who were the source of the channelings identified themselves as Matthew and Elliott. They described themselves as teachers and said that their work was in service to humanity.

After about a month with Matthew and Elliott, a new energy introduced itself by saying, "My name is John, and I have come to teach about self-love." The John energy alternated with Matthew and Elliott. Roseann could feel distinct differences between them.

She soon shared her meditation essays with a close friend, Noelle. Noelle liked them so much that she asked Roseann to channel for her. Soon a little group formed—Roseann, Noelle and her husband, Greg, and a few others. The group began meeting at Roseann's to hear channelings and discuss the material. They were told by their spirit advisers that, on a higher level of consciousness, they had volunteered to come together and work to bring others into the light. A book would come out of their work.

"It was incredible," said Roseann. "But it all unfolded just as they said it would. The channeled writing for every session began to form a story, a step-by-step progression for developing the inner self."

After a while, the spirit teachers Matthew, Elliott, and John announced that they would be leaving Roseann and would be replaced by another energy. "They told us that this was an angelic energy, the angels of light, and the angels were going to instruct us on a higher vibration," Roseann said. "Around Easter 1983, the first phase of the new energy came in for the first time. It was so loving—it was a love I'd never known on earth. It was very, very vast. I cried while I was writing, just because I was so loved. They called me "dear one" or "beautiful one," and it was so exalting."

The new energy remained with Roseann for two to three years, and then another change occurred. "The energy introduced itself as the Angels of Light and Truthful Revelation. They said that they were going to help us to reveal who we truly are in our daily lives, to bring all these teachings to an earthly form so that we could truly see ourselves and reveal ourselves and not be afraid to be chosen of light."

"This was a collective energy without personal names?" I asked.

"Yes. When the group first started, everyone wanted to know their guardian angel's name. At one meeting, I channeled all these names—some I could barely pronounce. Later on, as we grew, we were told that the name was like a key to tune in to the angel energy, but that where the angels are, there is such a oneness that individuality is not necessary. The energy is us as well—we are part of the angels, we are one with them.

"Let me explain it another way. Matthew, Elliott, and John were like teachers giving the information, whereas the angel energy is more experiential and loftier. I use the image of the mountain: with Matthew, Elliott, and John, we were on the lower part of the mountain, and with the angels, we were higher. It's an embracing energy that gives a sense of belonging. I believe that we're all one, anyway, and that we can, through love, be lifted up to a higher vibration, that which is who we truly are. The angels, in their lovingness of us, helped us to love ourselves. They gave us a mirror image of our unlimited selves."

"How have these experiences affected your life?" I asked.

"They changed everything. I had never felt that I could be loved so deeply, and this realization that I could was a great gift. I changed the way I saw myself and the way I saw other people. Where I used to be afraid to step into a room because I didn't know if I would be welcome, I know now that I am always welcome, that everything in that room is part of me, and everybody is a part of me.

"Another significant change was that I'm not judgmental anymore. There's just no way I can judge anybody, because in my eyes, everybody is loving. Now, I don't mean to sound as if I'm in denial of earthly realities. I'm not. I'm an alcohol counselor on the earth plane. I see things clearly. But that's not the only reality, and what I've learned is to speak in my heart. When I speak to others, I keep it in my heart that I am teaching to their higher self as well. There is a wisdom inside of each soul, a remembrance, and I feel that I'm here to help people remember that wisdom.

"These experiences made me belong to life," said Roseann. "I always used to feel separated, lonely, and lost, always needing to prove myself, or seek acceptance. Now I feel part of everything—part of the trees, part of the mountains, part of the people. Part of the best things that happen to me, and part of the worst things that happen. They're *all* part of me. By constantly loving it all, it gets transformed into love, which is a reflection of God."

Roseann said that some members of her immediate family were not able to understand the changes that had unfolded in her life, or the channelings. The breakup of her marriage also seemed to be part of her transformation, occurring at the time when Matthew, Elliott, and John were making their entrance. Matthew told her, "It is now your time to become a universal spirit, a universal soul. You have many to reach, and being with Peter is not where your life's path is anymore. You love him and he loves you, but it's time to separate."

"Even to this day, when people ask us why we got divorced, we say we don't really know. It's strange. There was never hostility. We just grew in different directions and had different things to do, though those things weren't manifested at that time. It was just the way it was supposed to be.

"I could never have done all this if we had stayed married. I wouldn't have had the lessons about being on my own and learning how to grow up and do all the things that I had always been so dependent on other people to do for me. I had to learn to rely on not only invisible help through the angels and guides but on the visible manifestation of that help. If you work hard enough on the invisible, it's got to manifest physically. It may take a little while, because it's much harder to change a physical reality than it is to change a thought. Physical changes start with thoughts, however."

The key to manifestation, said Roseann is "loving everything" in your life, everything that happens to you. Embracing it all and accepting it as part of your life experience. Then you can move on. "Trust whatever difficulty is manifesting," she said. "It's there for a reason, and the angels have helped us to accept everything as a friend. There are no enemies. If we think that an experience is our enemy, we're going to miss the boat, and it's going to become a greater enemy. But once you love it, it gets comforted.

"The angel teachings we've received help you to accept and integrate everything that happens to them. You have breathed these things into life! Nobody else did, you did! You can change things by the essence of your breath, which is your vital force. If you breathe anger, you will create angry situations. But if you breathe love—truly the breath of life—you create loving situations. The angels teach us that you are the conduit for the life force called God, and how you breathe it in and out will reflect in your reality."

I asked Roseann to describe the process by which she receives messages from the angels.

"It feels different, depending on whether I speak it or write it," she said. "When I speak it, I'm speaking and hearing at the same time, so it's like I become the words. It is one dance. I hear and feel everything I'm saying, even though I never know what I'm going to say. When I write it, it goes a little deeper into me, perhaps because I hear it in silence in my head.

"You see, if we separate ourselves from angels or from a voice of love, we're also separating ourselves from God. And we are not separate from God. We *are* God, sparks of God, so we are sparks of angels, we are sparks of each other. So we are one. We'll never get to know God as long as we think he's outside of us. Not only is God inside of us, but he *is* us. There are people who feel that angels and God are outside of them, and then there's the next step, those who know that they and the angels and God are one. I have had moments of knowing that oneness."

"That must be exquisite," I said.

"It's bliss. You are yourself and everything else at

the same time. Being everything, you know your individuality more. It's a strange experience.

"I've had two of these experiences. One was a dream. In the dream, I was in a hospital room, lying on a table. There were doctors with masks on. They were going to take a picture of me. When they went to shoot the camera, all of a sudden I experienced myself as a mass of loving energy. This was me, this was the picture. I was in such bliss that I was crying in the dream, and I woke up from it crying, because of the joy I felt. I was me and I was everything, and I was just massive energy. It was beautiful and special."

The second experience occurred when Roseann, Noelle, and Greg were in Maine hiking through forests down a mountain. Suddenly all three of them slipped into an expanded, timeless moment in which they felt themselves a part of the trees and everything around them. The experience altered Roseann's conscious point of view. "Trees have never been the same for me," she said. "Trees are me now, wherever I go."

Roseann said that one of the "high signs" that the angels gave her and her group was the number 22. In numerology, 22 is a master number, of high vibration. Their awareness of this secret sign of sorts came about through a series of synchronicities involving 22 and combinations of twos, such as $2.22 and 2:22 o'clock. When such numbers pop up spontaneously, they are taken as a sign that the angels are communicating their ongoing presence. For example, once Noelle wandered through a grocery store in a low state of mind, muttering to herself, "I am weary unto death, I am weary unto death." When she reached the checkout counter, her purchases totaled $2.22. It was a signal to her to snap out of her mood.

Once Roseann was to give a presentation to teachers and was assigned room number 222. She smiled to herself. The angels had the last laugh, for she discovered that there was no room 222. There was a 220 and a 221, but no 222. She was told it was a typing error, but Roseann felt there had been no mistake. The angels had given her the high sign to let her know that she was doing what she was supposed to be doing in life—a sort of "you're on the right track, and we're with you!"

(How curious that the angels working with Jane M. Howard selected August 22 as the date for Be An Angel Day. Jane and Roseann had never met.)

Death and Near-Death Apparitions

Angels stand by us throughout life. When our time comes to leave the earth plane, they assist us across the threshold to the next world.

The appearance of angels, spirits of the dead, or other spirit helpers at the time of death has been recorded throughout history. People who are conscious right before death sometimes exclaim on the sudden presence of a radiant deceased loved one, an angel, or another religious figure, such as Jesus or the Virgin Mary. Modern psychical researchers call such figures "deathbed apparitions" or "take-away apparitions." Around the turn of the twentieth century, psychical researchers began collecting anecdotal accounts of these figures. Most notable is the work done by William Barrett, an English professor of physics and one of the most famous early psychical researchers. Barrett became interested in deathbed apparitions because his wife was a doctor, and she heard numerous accounts of them in her work. He published a book on the subject, *Death-Bed Visions: The Psychical Experiences of the Dying,* in 1926.

Several decades later, two other researchers, Karlis Osis and Erlendur Haraldsson, both well known in parapsychology, added considerable material to the subject with the publication of their book, *At the Hour of Death.* Osis and Haraldsson examined tens of thousands of reports of deathbed apparitions collected in the United States and India.

Skeptics contend that such visions are due to lack of oxygen, hallucinations, drugs, disease, or depersonalization. Yet none of these possible explanations satisfactorily explains the visions. Furthermore, the visions are seen by the dying who are *not* heavily sedated or delirious but fully conscious.

Occasionally others can see the take-away angels as well. Shirley Steinhoff Cole, of Phoenix, Arizona, told me a story passed down to her by her mother, Louise Regina Beichner Steinhoff, about Shirley's grandmother, Mary Louise Cohlhepp.

"After all her children were grown [nine girls and four boys], all in good health, my grandmother became gravely ill and was taken to the hospital," Shirley said. "The doctors told my grandfather that his wife was gravely ill and was going to die, so they put her in what was called the death room. Her sons would hear of no such thing, so the four of them, against the wishes of her doctor, went into the hospital and carried her out, bed and all.

"When they got home, the girls nursed her back to health. Her hair had even turned white from the illness. When she was well again, her hair came in black as it was when she was young and healthy.

"She was very ill again at age sixty-six, and all the children were notified to come home to see their mother for the last time. They were all there in the room with her, when a band of angels surrounded her bed. Her soul left her body and the angels disappeared."

Perhaps all the children were blessed with witnessing the angels because they had been so close to, and caring for, their mother.

Similarly, persons who have near-death experiences (NDEs), in which they have clinical death and then are brought back, or return, to life, often report the same luminous figures. They travel down a tunnel toward a bright light, and sometimes are aware of being accompanied by beings of light or radiant spirits of the dead. When they reach a certain threshold, they may be told by these figures of light, or by voices they ascribe to angels, that they must return to life. Sometimes they are offered a choice: to return or to pass the point of no return to the other side.

Joy Snell, a former nurse in England, saw take-away apparitions frequently in her work in hospitals. She never told anyone what she saw lest they think she was crazy. After her retirement, she wrote about her experiences in a moving book, *The Ministry of Angels*. Sometimes she would see angels arrive at the bedside of someone who was on the brink of death, and stand by ready for the moment of transition. Immediately upon death, she would see the soul leave the body and coalesce into a spirit body just above the corpse. It would have the same radiance as that of the angels. Once the spirit body had formed, the angels would take it away. Snell longed to visit the place where they went, but was told by a disembodied, authoritative voice that she could not, for her work on earth was not finished. The true Other Side is not to be glimpsed by the living.

Snell also saw other apparitions in the course of her work. One was a ministering angel who took the form of a middle-aged female nurse. At first Snell thought this angel was in fact a human—just as Aimeé S. Lacombe had thought when she was rescued by the night nurse, as we saw in chapter 1. Joy would see this figure moving about wards only at night, simply touching sleeping or unconscious patients who had been in great pain and distress. Invariably, these patients reported the following morning that their pain was lessened or gone, or that they had experienced a profoundly restful night of sleep. Some said they'd had dreams in which they heard the most heavenly music. When Joy inquired who was this fabulous nurse who brought such relief to the patients, she discovered that no one on night duty matched the description.

Two others apparitions Snell saw were harbingers of death and life. The Angel of Death was a dark, shadowy, veiled figure that appeared at the foot of a patient's bed. No matter what the doctors said about the patient's chance for recovery, if the Angel of Death appeared, the patient always died within two to three days. Conversely, the Angel of Renewed Life forecast recovery. This angel appeared at the head of a patient's bed. He was a bright figure in a cloudlike, luminous robe, with a youthful, happy face. He always stood with his right arm raised and index finger pointing up, like a high sign. Again, no matter what the doctors said about the patient's chances of recovery—no matter how bleak—if the Angel of

Renewed Life manifested, the patient always recovered.

Angels make themselves known to us in whatever manner and form are the best in order to reach any one individual. If we are receptive and open-minded, some of our experiences may surprise us.

≡ 6 ≡

Give Me a Sign

As we've seen in other chapters, angels can intervene dramatically in our lives to save us from certain tragedy. Angels also can give us important information that can not only change our lives but the lives of other individuals as well.

Most often, angels work in more gentle and subtle ways, guiding us in our thoughts and deeds on a daily basis. These "little" interventions can have just as profound an effect on our beliefs and life philosophy as angel rescues. Such contact with angels can open us spiritually, steer us onto another course, or simply reaffirm that we're on the right track.

"What Should I Do?"

Leslie (a pseudonym) of McLean, Virginia, faced a crossroads in life at age twenty-three. She turned to God for help, and her guardian angel stepped in.

"I was at a very low point in my life," she said. "A relationship that I had thought would be permanent was ending, I hated my job, I didn't like my living arrangements, and a general dissatisfaction with my life was causing great despair. One cold November Sunday night I went to church. The auditorium was very large, seating between a thousand and two thousand people. On this night, attendance was sparse, and I sat on next to the last row with no one nearby. Waiting for the service to begin, I remember thinking to myself, 'God, what am I going to do?' A clearly audible voice said, 'Go back to school.' The voice was so clear I turned around to see who sat behind me. To my surprise, there was no one there.

"I had never considered returning to school as a possible response to my situation, but the advice made such good sense that I quit my job, stored my furniture, and within three months was back in college as a full-time student. The fact that I had only seven hundred dollars to my name never seemed like an impediment, and of course, it wasn't. I was able to get loans and find jobs and assistantships all the way through my master's degree. Sometimes the work came in ways that were truly miraculous. My guardian angel seemed to be working overtime.

"The truly amazing aspect of this experience was that I did not think it unusual or strange in any way. I never told anyone of the experience until years later, after I had become involved in a spiritual search. Only then did I truly recognize how I had been blessed, and I was amazed that I had the good sense to follow the guidance. I am very happy that I listened and acted."

In a similar at-a-crossroads situation, an angel manifested visibly to Phyllis Montgomery of Santa

Fe, New Mexico, and her young son. The experience is unusual, in that the apparition appeared to both of them at about the same time but while each was in a separate location.

Said Phyllis, "In 1984, I decided, very precipitously and most uncharacteristically for me, to take advantage of a new house I could rent in Santa Fe. Overnight, I made a plan to take a self-proclaimed 'sabbatical' and run away from New York City with my then eleven-year-old son. As we approached the departure date, I was racked with anxiety about the wisdom of my decision and how it would affect my young son being at such a distance from his father and his friends.

"One night, close to the date to leave, I tossed and turned all night. At four A.M., I decided to get up to do some yoga exercises to try to relax, because I had a very full agenda for the next day. I was in a shoulder stand when I realized that an angel was suspended midair in my living room. My perception was that it was feminine and she was glowing in a light of luminescent white-gold. Although I did not 'hear' as one normally hears, I heard the message 'Do not be afraid, you and your son are being led.' Then she was gone.

"I rushed to my meditation seat in the hopes of trying to reconnect with this angel. I glanced at the living room clock. It was 4:45 A.M. I was not quite settled into my seat when I heard my son's footsteps. I was stunned because he *never* awoke during the course of the night. As he approached me, he said, 'Mom, I just had an apparition.' I said I had had one also, and asked him to tell me about his. He said that there was a figure in his room, and while he could not see all the features clearly, he thought it was a woman. He then tried to describe luminescence by saying she was surrounded by a strange light, and that she had her arm outstretched and was pointing her finger. He indicated that he 'heard' her say, 'Go!' though it wasn't a voice he could describe.

"I asked him to show me which direction her arm was stretched. It was west."

Sealed with the Holy Spirit

If ever anyone needed an angelic high sign, it was Edith S. of Swannanoa, North Carolina. The time was 1972. Edith, a devout Christian, had been struggling for years to cope with serious family problems.

"Have you ever heard of the statement 'Being born of food that has been much tried by fire'?" Edith began. "Well, in a spiritual sense, it means a person such as I, who has had to go through an awful lot of tragedies and negative situations in life, and in spite of it all, still desires to become the person the Lord wants them to be.

"As a child, I came from a broken home, with a family history filled with self-destructive people through suicides, alcoholism, and murder. In going through all these negative experiences, with the family members bent on destroying themselves and those around them, I realized that the only *true* 'parent' I could depend upon was God the Father Almighty. Even though I did feel like an orphan, having to be in and out of a children's home quite often due to family tragedies, I always knew that even though I felt like there was no one else there for me, there was always God.

"Being unfamiliar with the many guises of alcoholism, I ended up marrying an alcoholic in 1968. My then-husband was a *constant* beer drinker, but it never dawned on me that the problems in our relationship were due to the fact that he was an alcoholic. As you can well imagine, I was living through a hellish situation, with his playing all sorts of psychological and emotional warfare to keep a wall between us. Until I came upon Al-Anon, I truly believed that the problems were due to *me.* That was not the case at all, even though my alcoholic husband tried his hardest to make *me* look like the bad guy all the time.

"You can believe me when I tell you that in spite of all I was going through, I was very close to God. With my own mother committing suicide over my errant father, I kept praying to God to help make me the person he wanted me to be, in spite of everything. I told God that I did not want to commit suicide like my mother did to escape her situation from my father. I prayed constantly to God to *please help me,* even going into the closet and pouring my heart out to him with tears just streaming down my face.

"Then one summer night, *it happened!* A new bedroom and bathroom addition had just been completed on our home, and my first daughter was at the other end of the house in the old bedroom. With her being just eighteen months old and still apt to wake up and cry during the night, I naturally wanted to be able to hear her cries. So I purchased a plug-in intercom system. One was in her room, set permanently on the 'talk' position, and mine was set next to my side of the bed on the table, permanently set on the 'listen' position. This worked quite well, for the intercom also put out a faint light that served as a night light for me when I had to get up in the middle of the night to attend to her.

"One June night in 1972, my husband and I had gone to bed. I was pregnant with my second daughter, who was due in December. I had closed my eyes but had not yet gone to sleep. Suddenly I heard a voice doing mumbling or chanting of some sort. I immediately opened my eyes, because I thought it was my eighteen-month-old daughter starting to wake up and cry, and I would have to attend to her.

"I was lying on my back and I did not expect to see what I saw! Above me, there appeared to be someone who looked female floating above me. She was chanting something in a language I had never heard, and all the while was moving her right hand across my forehead. I looked to the right side of my bed, and standing there was what appeared to be someone male. He was wearing a white robe. I quickly looked him up and down. There were long sleeves on his robe, and at the end of each sleeve were two bands of gold trim.

"My eyes kept moving from the being above me to the one beside my bed. The standing one had his hands folded in front of him, his right hand over his left. He appeared to be dark-haired with dark eyes. He had such a wonderful expression on his face, as though he knew something I did not at the time. No words were spoken. I thought to myself, 'Are you from outer space?' In just a few minutes, the whole episode was over. The shock of what happened got me out of bed to go think about it.

"After that, I read some books on angels and

consulted with some Christian clergymen, trying to find out what the experience signified. With the spiritual insight I had after the experience, I knew that the Lord had sent those angels as a visible sign to me to let me know that he was sealing me with his Holy Spirit, and the angel above me was writing the Lord's name upon my forehead. I belonged to Him! And, he wanted me to be a witness to the sealing of his Holy Spirit upon me as an assurance to me, because he must have known that I needed that assurance. The clergymen weren't able to help me. They were only able to tell me that there are angels that God sends to aid those who are to receive salvation."

Minding Morals

Bob (a pseudonym) is a retired officer of the U.S. Air Force. He grew up an Episcopalian and throughout most of his life never gave much thought to angels, though he did feel uncommonly protected and lucky. In the early 1970s, while on a trip for the Air Force to Addis Ababa, Ethiopia, he had the first of some experiences that changed his mind about angels and had other, far-reaching effects as well.

"I was staying in the Hilton Hotel, and I went to my room," Bob told me. "There was a knock on the door, and suddenly there was one of the most beautiful women I've ever seen in my life standing there, very seductively. She had long blond hair and looked like the actress Barbara Eden. I was startled—she was so beautiful. I'd seen her around the hotel and had had some conversations with her. She invited me into her room. I was married—and still am—but I was torn, and was tempted to go. I declined her offer and she left. I wondered, did I make the right choice? Even though I love my wife, at the same time I was certainly tempted. My room had a Bible in it, and I started reading it and thinking about that aspect of life.

"When I got back home to the States a couple of days later, I was still thinking about all this as I drove home from the base. I hope this doesn't sound silly, but I was questioning, is there a God, and are there angels. As I was driving along, I said, 'God, if you're real, give me a sign!' No sooner had I said the words than a brilliant light came right at the windshield almost into the car. It was like a flash of lightning or a flashbulb going off right in front of me. I was so startled that I almost couldn't believe that it happened. I thought maybe I imagined the whole thing.

"At home, I was greeted by my wife and kids, and I assured myself that I'd done the right thing back in Addis Ababa. I know it may sound obvious to you, but I grew up in a *Playboy* atmosphere where taking advantage of such a situation was considered the thing to do.

"When I went to sleep that night, I was visited by a figure that I can only describe as an angel. I don't know whether I dreamed it, or I awoke and saw it in the bedroom. It was a shining white figure, a huge, tall man in robes, a very loving figure, just radiating love. He walked to the side of my bed and put his hand on me. He didn't say anything, but I got the impression that he was telling me that I had done a good job—the right thing."

"Could you see his face?" I asked.

"Yes, it was like I would expect an angel to look like.

It seemed Scandinavian in appearance, very fair. It was glowing.

"When he touched my arm, I could feel a lot of love and warmth, and a feeling that he loved me. After I received this message, the figure just disappeared. It was certainly a religious experience! And it was real—as real as anything else in my life."

"How did the experience affect you?" I said.

"I was more convinced than ever that there is a God and that his guardian angels do exist," Bob answered. "Afterward, I started reading about angels to find out more about them. I felt more of a connection to religion and had more interest in attending church. I became much closer to God. I was stimulated to study about other religions. I decided I was most comfortable with Christianity, but I could see the parallels among the different religions. Another thing that happened to me was that I became much more aware of the earth. I became active as an environmentalist in my town.

"I definitely believe that God has a plan for us," Bob continued. "In fact, there are some indications that the angels are in control. I don't necessarily mean that they decide every little thing that happens to us, but they're here in large numbers, and guarding us. What they decide is how the world goes. Conversely, there are the fallen angels who are trying to make bad things happen. They control some people, too. Various religions have the apocryphal story that there will be a great battle between good and evil."

I asked Bob if he thought the figure was his guardian angel, and he shook his head. "I didn't get a sense of that, but I feel this angel is still around me. I feel that in times of trouble I can call on him. It gives me a lot of peace."

It's the Right Thing to Do

Jane M. Howard is often given guidance by angels that she does not fully understand at the time. However, she long ago learned to trust the guidance, and so she follows it when it is given. Time and time again, what the angels say bears out. Sometimes, what she is guided to do has a great impact on another person, which Janie herself could not have foreseen.

"I received a jewelry catalog in the mail, and in that catalog I saw a pair of simulated diamond earrings in the shape of dear little angels," she told me. "I heard my guardian angel tell me that I should buy these earrings. I questioned that message, even though these were truly precious, because I have a pair of diamond studs that my boyfriend, Walt, gave me for Christmas two years earlier, and I never take them out. I adore them! I could not fathom that I would ever wear these earrings in the catalog. However, I heard loud and clear that I was to buy them, and so I did.

"The earrings arrived and sat in their little gift box on my dresser for about a month. Then one day I received a phone call from a close friend in New York. This wonderful woman had just returned from the doctor's office, where she had been told that she had cancer of the uterus. She was so frightened by the bleak prognosis. And she was very confused about decisions she had to make, and she knew she had to make them quickly. She asked if I would pray for her, and I told her I would begin immediately.

"When I hung up the phone at my desk at the advertising agency where I work, and had got up from my chair, I felt myself encircled by the most loving angels of service, who were chiming to me in unison that I needed to go home at lunchtime and package up the earrings—they were for this woman to wear. They were to be sent to her immediately as a gift from the angels with this message: when she wore them, the angels would be there whispering in her ears, 'We love you. It's going to be all right. Don't be frightened. We are here with you. You are not alone.' The angels added that I was to tell this woman that she was to wear these earrings in 'good health,' because that was what the angels were sending her—blessings of good health. And so I followed those instructions and the earrings were on their way to New York.

"Several days later, I received a call from my friend. She stated that the earrings had arrived on a day when she was having a battery of exams and tests, and they were truly a gift of strength from heaven. My friend commented that this had been one of the lowest days in her life until the angelic gift of love arrived. She felt the earrings were truly a miracle. She has since shared with me the inspiration that the earrings have given her to face the challenges at this time. The angels constantly reassure her by the presence of the 'angelic present' that she is not alone, and to open herself to the gifts of heaven, which include healing—and sometimes even a pair of earrings!"

═══ 7 ═══

Cupid Calls

The threat of disaster and tragedy or a great need to influence others are not the only reasons that bring angels swooping into our lives. Angels orchestrate synchronicities and circumstances that bring us opportunities meant for us on our life's path. It is up to us to recognize the opportunities and seize them.

Angels can help us find contentment, fulfillment, and happiness. Sometimes that means meeting the right person, as the following story shows.

Ray and Kathleen are the sweetest pair of lovebirds you'll ever find. There is no other way to describe them. They are totally in love with each other, and live totally for each other. They say angels brought them together, and angels continue to grace their love. Ray and Kathleen shared their experiences with me over a sweethearts' brunch on, appropriately, Valentine's Day. We met in a suburb of Washington, D.C.

Before Ray and Kathleen met, Kathleen had reached the low point of her life. She had struggled to survive for twenty-seven years in a destructive marriage that took a heavy emotional toll. With two children at home, she felt trapped. She had nowhere to turn for support, nowhere to go.

"I was married to a dominating man," Kathleen said. "I fought for equality in my marriage and never was able to achieve it. The lack of equality and respect destroyed the very foundation of our relationship. I can't believe I'm part of that cliché about people staying together for their kids, but that's what I did. I stayed when the pain for myself was awful. I couldn't dissociate from it. Until I literally left my home, I could not understand the incredible emotional bind that I was in. My husband had ahold of my heart, and I couldn't see it until I got out of it. It's called abuse, and that was a word that was not in my vocabulary until recently. I didn't understand that the things he was doing and saying to me were abuse.

"I felt increasingly paralyzed in the last five to six years. I had become more introspective. I had a sense of hopelessness, a lack of a future. I felt deep inadequacies about myself, that I was never going to be good enough, that I was never going to find something creative in life, that past talents were dead or didn't amount to anything. I had a feeling that I had no power in my life, that I was crippled, that I couldn't make a difference. No matter what I did in my marriage, nothing changed. I was dead-ended. An image that came to me of my marriage was of a long hallway, and all the doors were shut. Nothing was at the end."

The notion that God might intervene in her life, or send his angels to do so, didn't occur to Kathleen. She had never given angels much thought. The conditions of her marriage caused her to wither spiritually. "It was my theory that there is a Creator, but he does not put his finger into our lives," she said. "That would trivialize him. People who thought their lives were so important that their prayers would be answered— well, I thought that was a fallacy."

In agony over her marriage, Kathleen sought help from various individuals. One was a minister. Once while talking with her, Kathleen had an extraordinary experience. Suddenly she felt a presence that was like a light streaming toward her. It was so profound that she began shaking. The minister told her it was a sign, a facilitator, a signal. But even though she knew she had to take action to alleviate her pain, Kathleen could not yet summon her resolve. She was like thousands of others who find themselves trapped in desperate circumstances—afraid that letting go of one bad situation would only bring on a worse one. Fear of the unknown, a paralyzer.

Meanwhile, in another state not far away, Ray was living a life that was not dire but stagnant emotionally and spiritually.

"I was never happy in my marriage," Ray said. "I was emotionally hungry, and I didn't find what I was looking for. My wife and I started drifting apart the same year we were married. But we kept things going on an even keel until about 1960, then they started to fall apart. We stayed together—we had three beautiful boys."

Ray eventually moved out and went to work in

another state. He and his wife remained married, but they lived completely separate lives. Ray had other relationships, but none worked out for the long term.

"I've always been searching for that relationship that most of us know in our hearts must exist," he said. "But we tend to take second best, because that is what we find there on the plate. We don't think to keep looking for the best. People look at what comes along, at what's been given to them on their plate and say, well, this doesn't look bad, it isn't exactly what I ordered, but I'll eat it, anyway. But what they're waiting for is that plate that blows everything else out of the water and is just sugar plums and angel dust. That's what you've got to hold out for. If you get sidetracked, you waste years looking for that love you really want.

"So, I was keeping very busy with work, but I was very empty in one part—I had no one to share my love of nature with, my love of writing with. I had fame and money, but they don't count. I wanted more than that."

Unlike Kathleen, who'd had no prior experience of angels, Ray had been visited by an angel as a child. "My parents were very abusive toward me—I was always getting flogged and horsewhipped," he said in a matter-of-fact tone. "On this occasion, my father had been enjoying himself whipping me. I must have been eight or nine. I was put to bed crying. I lay there for a long while, and then I felt a sudden peace come over the room. There was a person standing over the bed looking at me very sadly. A person dressed in Middle East garb. I assumed it was male, but I didn't know for sure. He was not exactly transparent, but not flesh-and-blood, either. I stopped crying. He put his hands out, looked at me, and slowly vanished. My reaction was that he was Jesus or an angel. The feeling from the figure was extreme love and caring. Ever since then, I've assumed that because I had that visitation, I've had a charmed life."

It's not uncommon for two people to meet and fall in love, and say to each other, especially if they are in midlife, "Where were you years ago? Why didn't I meet you first, and avoid all that pain?" There is a purpose to everything, even pain. Ray and Kathleen know that we are guided to meet others when the time is right. We must be prepared and ready to be open to the opportunities. They know that they may not have been able to appreciate each other had it not been for their respective life experiences. And, they know that one should never look back but keep moving forward.

The couple met at a computer conference in 1990. Nothing much happened. A year later, at the same computer conference, they were ready for change and ready for each other. The angels were busy pushing them together. A friend of Kathleen's called her attention to Ray, and pointed out that they had similar interests.

At lunchtime at the conference, Kathleen approached Ray and said, "What are you doing later this afternoon? I'm going to be taking that boat trip up the river."

Ray looked at her and said, "What am I going to be doing this afternoon? I'm going to be lifting weights." Hardly a romantic opening.

Kathleen persevered. "What are you going to be doing later on tonight?"

Ray then gave an answer that surprised him: "I'm going to be in the lobby at seven-thirty, and I'd like to take you to dinner." Kathleen smiled.

Ray then picked up the story: "We went to dinner at a place where we'd been before, where most of the people from the conference were going. We sat across from each other and I never looked at anything else but Kathleen the whole time. All I looked at was her beautiful face. I never took my eyes off her face, and she never took her eyes off of me. We talked, and as we talked we fell in love in a way that I thought was not possible. I never thought that anything like that would happen to me. I thought she was charming, intelligent, lovely, and so beautiful, not just her exterior but in her soul as well."

"This is the most wonderful man that I've ever known in my whole life," chimed in Kathleen. "The kindest, the gentlest. I can't believe how sensitive he is, how tuned in to me. He works at trying to please me. It's overwhelming, something I thought I never would experience."

They went to their separate rooms that night, but neither one could sleep all night long. "I felt something was moving my life," Kathleen said. "All I could think of was love. We had discussed writing to each other, and it was such a remarkable coincidence that both of us wanted to write to another person and have it be meaningful—neither of us had had that experience. We started writing to each other, and this has promoted and enhanced our love right from the beginning. When I write to Ray, I open my soul and pour it out to him."

They met again two months later and consummated their love. "The first time we made love, even though we knew what sex was all about, we knew that this was something different from anything we had ever experienced in our lives before," said Ray. "Everything we knew about sex meant absolutely nothing. It was as if a door had opened. This was for us the very first time either of us had made love. It was a completely new and very wonderful experience. It's transcended everything I've ever known about this world. We've been guided by angels and loving spirits who want us to experience the vitality of love such as very few humans are privileged to experience."

For Kathleen, it marked a dramatic turning point. "I was suddenly awakened to incredible needs in myself," she said. "Needs that hadn't been met in my destructive marriage. It was the greatest pain in my life to make that decision to leave my marriage, but I was finally able to say that I deserved to be happy. I saw that I was staying in the marriage out of fear, and that scared me. I could not go on living the way I was living, because that would be a lie. I could not face the rest of my life living as though I were in prison. So, I chose life rather than death. The other way, I was definitely dying.

"Ray told me, 'Life is very full, Kathleen.' Suddenly I was hearing the most refreshing, wonderful thing. I was excited by it. It set off bells in my head. I knew intuitively that I was with somebody who was not going to take from me. The relationship I'd been in was annihilating me. I didn't have anything more to give. Ray has never taken—he helps me to give more."

But Ray did not sweep Kathleen away to a castle. They lived, after all, in separate states. They had jobs in separate states. They had personal affairs to wrap up. For Kathleen, she also knew that she had to stand on her own two feet. With the support of her friends and counselors, she found an apartment and began living by herself. It's a modest but happy home, and she feels she was guided to be there. She and Ray began a courtship that includes daily phone calls, frequent letters, and frequent visits.

Ray and Kathleen feel so blessed that they are certain it was angels who brought them together. "It's uncanny," said Ray. "I think the angels are rejoicing that we are together and are planning more adventures for us. They have a way of making things work out for us."

When the two of them are together, especially after they have made love, they experience something extraordinary: a sense of a great aura of loving energy around them.

In addition, Kathleen has been blessed by visions, which she feels are brought by the angels. The visions arise spontaneously, and are of beautiful scenes, such as sunsets, or of tropical birds. The colors are brilliant and vibrant, alive with energy, unlike anything she has ever seen on earth. "I see these visions as an indication that Ray and I should be connected," said Kathleen. "One vision was astonishing in its direct link to him. It happened on a weekend that we had been together. It was in the morning. Ray had gotten up and had taken a shower. I wasn't really asleep. I had my eyes closed. He came to the bed and reached out his hand and touched me. I saw this vision when he touched me and it was mauve roses coming at me. I opened my eyes and he said, 'You will let me take care of you, won't you?' I said, 'Of course.' Then I had an incredible need to shut my eyes again, that there was something unfinished. I shut my eyes and saw a bouquet of mauve roses coming at me. I associated the flowers with his care for me."

Kathleen said her visions were not fleeting but lingered for a long time. She had the ability to leave them and reenter them. They were vivid, and not dreamlike. "Many of them have a repeated theme, almost always of nature, such as dense green foliage and vibrant, tropical flowers," she said. "I've had many visions of waterfalls, pools and trees and vines. And vibrant flowers, bright red, and also purple, one of the predominant colors. One vision came while we were in a park, leaning up against a tree, kissing and caressing very sensuously. With my eyes closed, I saw a magnificent vision of deep purple-blue mountains against a sunset of violent orange. Two days later we went to the Blue Ridge Mountains, and I was amazed to see a sunset similar to the one in my vision. Another time, one evening after making love, I saw a surrealistic, swirling ribbon of many colors. It seemed to represent the emotional, physical side of our love."

The visions and the auras, she said, bring "a feeling of moving into another realm because of our love. It's more than pure emotion. It's totally transcendent, for we're divorced from reality. We do actually enter some other place of colors and aromas. Ray and I are connected, but we have no form. The physical world around us ceases to exist, and we're surrounded by incredible beauty on all sides." The auras, she said, have a "tremendous power that emanates from a center that is golden and silver with flashes of aqua."

"We fill whatever space we're in," said Ray. "The

love that we have, which is represented by golden light, we're at the center of it. We fill this universe, whatever it is. It's beautiful. Nothing else matters. I love her totally and completely, with all my heart and with all my soul, forever and ever. This is another one of the gifts that has been given to us by the angels."

Said Kathleen, "The intensity of our relationship enables us to reach something that is eternal."

Both Kathleen and Ray feel they are being guided by powerful forces. The angels have much in store for them, discoveries they have yet to make. They are both energized by their love—they feel filled with a new creative energy that enables them to do everything they did before, and more. "The love that Kathleen and I have is worth more than all the gold in the world," said Ray. "Money, gold, silver, jewels, possessions, don't matter. Once you're in love, everything suddenly comes into perspective."

"One of the most damaging things about my marriage was that I could not share my soul," Kathleen said. "If you can't share your soul, then you're only acting out an existence rather than truly living. I think angels can precipitously change people's lives, and they choose people for that very carefully. I think they chose us to be brought together about two years ago. They worked everything out so we were in the right jobs at the right time at the right place. Then they took hold of both of us and shook us and said, *Wake up!*"

She went on, "The angels have not taken anything away, except fear, uncertainty, loneliness, the negative parts of life. Desperation. Despondency. They've replaced them with love, caring, affection, spiritual development, mental development, learning, happiness, enjoyment of nature, the total enjoyment of being in love and being alive."

Ray said that although angels can give people great help, he did not think that appealing to them alone could have accounted for the relationship. "There had to be another hand in it," he said. "I don't know whose. A strong, loving hand had to bring our life lines together and guide us from that time on. The angels are the instruments of that hand, and they are always with us. When we part the angels cry, as we do. The angels are extremely happy when we meet. They're holding us together. I don't see angels as entities but as something very powerful that interacts in our lives in the most benevolent ways, to give Kathleen especially some very beautiful insight into the spirit world through her visions. They've enabled me to say and do things and I don't know where they've come from.

"I've never wanted anything from Kathleen, I've never demanded anything, never pressed her for anything. That has been reinforced by the angels—that I am to love her, serve her, protect her. Our love is a precious flower beyond all expectations. We have a love that literally knows no bounds. At times, when we experience this fourth dimension, our love is really expanded beyond the limits of the known universe."

Lucky people, Ray and Kathleen. They have been blessed by the angels, and their thanks for the blessings bring them even greater blessings.

Kathleen has been inspired to write poetry to Ray. Here is what she wrote for Valentine's Day 1992:

My sweet, sweet love
Resplendent with aromatic spices and azure skies
Of golden kisses ripe with the sun's rich glow
The warmth of a rosy aura
Holds our souls in rapture
Folds us in a rich velvet cocoon.
Your presence strikes the hidden pulse
In my throat and sets myself on fire.
In the warm enclosure of your arms
I unfold like the silky petals of the rose,
Caught in the early summer shower
Of crystal beads and honeyed hours.
As I open to your fervent touch
A lute song echoes across the narrowing space
Transfixing us in the love we create.

8

In Search of Angels and Souls of the Dead

If you wish to contact the soul of someone on the Other Side, or communicate with angels or other beings, or cure a place of being haunted, your best bet is Eddie Burks. Eddie is renowned in England as a clairvoyant, medium, and healer. He is especially famous for his effective work in releasement, which is helping souls who are trapped on the earth plane to move on to the next world. The work requires a collaboration between Eddie and a host of assisting spirits and angels.

How Eddie came into his talent, and how he uses it, is quite a story. When I met him in England, he was living and working at Inlight House, a small retreat center near the elegant little village of Grayshott in Hampshire. The setting was fairy-tale—a tidy brick country house with a fresh appearance, set on lovely, landscaped private grounds next to a government-owned forest trust. Eddie had instilled within the house a soothing energy. At night, especially when the moon rode high in the sky, the woods and lawn were full of dancing fairies and nature spirits. It was a magical place, and it was there that Eddie connected me to angels and devas in a way I had never before experienced.

Eddie's first peek into the world of spirits came at an early age:

"I had a near-death experience at the age of five or six, coming out of an operation for a tonsillectomy," he told me. "This was in London—I was born in the east end. During this near-death experience, I went somewhere wonderful—I just can't tell you how wonderful that was. Coming back, I felt myself hurtling along a tunnel. I was very, very upset, angry even, that I'd been taken away from somewhere that was so wonderful that I couldn't bear to leave it. This tunnel experience haunted me for years. I dreamed about it about once a month until the age of thirty. It was more of a nightmare, because I was so angry at having been torn away from this place. Disappointed like a little child would be. When I was thirty, I read about the tunnel experience for the first time, and was able to put the experience into context and realize what it was all about. And I never dreamt about it any more after that, because I'd now dealt with it."

"Did that experience influence your later psychic awareness?" I asked.

"Oh, yes," Eddie agreed. "It actually set me on the road, got me searching. But the effect it had immediately on me [as a child] was that I realized that they were not telling us the truth in Sunday school. They were teaching us about the New Testament, but they never told us what I had experienced. They were missing this great big piece that was so important. This is what I wanted to know more about, and I couldn't find it in the church.

"So I started to look for the truth as soon as I was old enough to be able to do that. I read philosophy at the ages of eleven and twelve, thinking that I would find this truth that I knew was there but I couldn't reach. I discovered that philosophy was barren as far as that search was concerned. Then one day, while still roaming through the library books in the local library, I came across a book called *Encyclopedia of Psychic Science,* with a foreword by Sir Oliver Lodge, and I knew I was home. I got interested through that in the Spiritualist movement, and that was an interest that came and went. I was in the army four and a half years, and then after the war [World War II] there was a period where I wasn't active in the spiritual field because I was bringing up a family and making a career as a civil engineer. It wasn't until 1970, when my first wife died unexpectedly at age fifty-one and then came back to me posthumously a number of times, that my awareness began to show itself. In 1981, my only son and only child by my first marriage dropped dead in the same way as had my wife, with a burst aortal artery. He was thirty-five. The events around that left me no doubt about survival after death. It was a repeat of what had happened with my wife, but stronger."

"How did your wife and son come back?" I asked.

"Margaret—we called her Peggy—came back the day after she died. My son had come back to the house from Derby, which was about twenty-five miles from where I was living, to be with me. We were both feeling utterly miserable. Lunchtime came and I said we must eat something. So I took out of the refrigerator a chicken I had shared with my wife the day before, and there was some of it left over. My son was standing near me, and I was morosely cutting up this chicken, and suddenly I burst out laughing. My son thought that I'd flipped. I said, 'It's all right, it's all right, Michael. Your mother is here and she is reminding me about what happened yesterday.' And she was. She was reminding me that I'd cut chicken up the day before, put all the good bits on her plate, scruffy bits on mine, and the two plates somehow got interchanged, and I had all the good stuff and she had all the poor bits. We laughed about it at the time. She was using this event to lift me out of my sadness, you see. From that point on, I felt so different. I was walking on air. She kept coming back and I knew she was around. I knew she had survived. I couldn't see her, but I got a lot of information telepathically from her. That went on quite some time.

"At the time he died, Michael was living in Scotland, where he had gone to get a job. He was living with a girl he was hoping to marry, his first marriage having broken up. When the lady concerned phoned me to let me know that he died, I went straight up by train. The following morning I went out to get a death certificate. When I went back into the house, she was busy at the kitchen sink. And as I walked into the room, it was as though I had walked into Michael. I said to her, 'Good heavens, Michael's here.' She didn't even turn round. She said, 'I know he is. I've been talking to him.' She's psychic, too, but she had repressed it for a number of years. Her psychism was resurrected by his death. Michael was with us a number of times in the days that followed. When I returned five days later to my home in Nottinghamshire, I again felt his presence and continued to feel his presence on and off for quite a time, then less frequently as time passed. But I was never thinking that I was bringing him back. He was coming back out of sheer love, I think, because we were very close."

Peggy's presence also diminished over time—both she and her son were evolving in their own right on the Other Side. "Three or four months after my wife died, I went to the Norfolk coast for a weekend merely to relive the memories of a holiday we had a fortnight before she died. I was rather disappointed because I was unaware of her over that weekend. I felt sure she would make an appearance, but she didn't. So I got in the car to come back. It's a three-hour journey. As soon as I sat in the car, she was in the passenger's seat at the side of me. We held a mental conversation for an hour and a half. At the end of it she said, 'I have to go now, and you won't be hearing from me for some time.' In an instant she'd gone. I didn't hear from her for a long while. I feel sure that during that period, she went through the self-judgment. When she next contacted me, I could feel there was a difference—she was more etherealized somehow. She's come back at widely spaced intervals since.

"At the end of 1974 to early 1975, I was suddenly pitched into healing work. It was spontaneous. As I developed the healing, doors opened in my awareness, and I would find myself involved in other aspects of the person's life.

"For about six years before this, I'd been aware of a

presence with me, and it would come to me at any time. I might be driving, I might be watching television, I might be reading, I might be at my office desk. It was benign, and I knew it could be trusted. It brought me a great feeling of uplift and peace.

"I could sense it, but I couldn't hear it or see it. I could sense it, sense it very strongly. It was nearly always on my right side, somewhere behind me. Quite close up, almost like a cloud hovering there."

The first indication that the spirit had arrived to help Eddie become a healer happened spontaneously. "One day I went to see a friend whose wife had just come out of the hospital after having a severe spinal operation. I went on the spur of the moment. Five minutes before I got there, she got out of bed for the first time since she returned from hospital, put her dressing gown on, and sat in the living room, as though she were expecting me. I tried to start a conversation with her, but I realized she was too weak. So I started to talk past her, toward her husband. She suddenly intervened and said, 'Have you brought a spiritual presence into the room?' The moment I acknowledged it, I simply had to get up and take her hands, and whoosh! something happened. A surge of wonderful power or energy just flowed straight through me toward her. I'd never had this happen before."

"What was your reaction?" I asked.

"Amazement, absolute amazement. It was as though a switch was thrown. A fortnight later, at the age of nearly seventy, she was dancing on the patio in the back garden to show me how quickly she'd recovered. She was going out shopping. She lived for another seven or eight years. From that day on, I've been coming across people that I have to help."

One person Eddie helped was a woman who was diagnosed with uterine cancer. He gave her healing prior to her entering the hospital for radiation treatment and a hysterectomy. During the healing, he saw a light shining at the end of a tunnel and was told that he wasn't to say anything about it.

Eddie visited the woman several days after the operation. She was sitting up beaming. "The sister is amazed at the way I've come through it," she told Eddie. "But we know why, don't we?"

"Yes, we do," Eddie responded.

"I've still got to learn the results of the tests they've done to find out whether I have any malignant cells floating about me," she said.

"You'll find it's clear," Eddie said, thinking of the light at the end of the tunnel.

Sure enough, no malignancy was detected. After several months, the woman was well enough to return to work. She learned to drive a car for the first time, and embarked on a life full of activity.

As time went on, Eddie experienced an increasing inner urge to help people with healing. People would come to his house after work, as many as seven in an evening. Eddie did laying on of hands, following his intuition. Eventually the healing work expanded to include the releasement of earthbound souls.

He sometimes receives direction from nonphysical beings, without knowing who they are. "I'm sure there is an angelic presence, and I always invoke an angelic presence," he said. I ask in a silent blessing that I give at the end of each healing for the angelic being most linked with that person to be able to draw close and give guidance and help in whatever way is necessary. I'm much less specific in my healing now, because I've come to realize, as most healers do after a time, that we don't know enough to be specific about how the healing should be applied. Some people need their illness, for example, and it's not up to us to intervene to take that illness away. It's really part of their karmic past, and they must deal with it. So I try to make my healing nonspecific, and hand over to whatever presence is with me, including the angelic presence that I always feel is close."

Eddie said that he senses a Native American presence with him. "I think the reason why so many people working in this field think they have red Indian guides or helpers is because this is the one race that we most need for their experience at this time," he said.

Eddie is both clairsentient and clairvoyant. I asked Eddie to describe his process of tuning in to higher dimensions.

"I suppose the nearest description I can give is that I allow no force, but I allow my consciousness to respond to a different level. It's a tuning, and sometimes it has to be a fairly fine tuning. I am aware sometimes of tuning in to much higher levels than others. It's as though my consciousness goes into a lift or an elevator. In some subtle way the elevator goes up, taking my conscious with it, and knows the level at which it has to stop. How it does it, I don't know. But I'm more and more conscious of the immense powers of the mind and the fact that we are only just touching on the edge of it. I don't try to do this—using willpower wouldn't do any good. Trying it out of curiosity wouldn't work either. It seems to be the result of a purposeful desire to do something for others.

"I remember looking for a man, a suicide. In an instant the feeling I had was that some part of my mind was sweeping round, almost like a searchlight. Within seconds it located this man. How it really did it, I don't know—I only get an impression. Someone who has passed over recently is much easier to find than someone who went on, say, a couple of years ago. They are at much different levels.

"If I go too far, I feel as though an elastic band inside my brain on my right side is being stretched. It's a physical discomfort, a warning sign, and I know that I mustn't go beyond that. That is the nearest physical effect I get. Something else worth mentioning: if I'm approached by an entity that is good, then the approach seems to be made from the right-hand side. On the rare occasions I'm approached by an entity that's evil—and most of them, fortunately, don't seem to be able to break through my defenses—then they come on the left side. So, for me, the left is the bad, the right is good. When I'm moving up in consciousness, I'm moving into a brighter light. And light and spiritual heights are synonymous, the same way that evil and darkness are synonymous. Maybe not synonymous, but they almost interchange. But light and love, darkness and hatred seem to hold to each other, very clearly."

Eddie often gets clairvoyant impressions when he works with earthbound souls, some of whom have been stuck for centuries. "I often see the costume they're wearing, which gives me a very good idea of what period of history they belong to," he said. "This impression is often confirmed in other ways. I see them after I've been through the initial stages of catharsis with them. I see someone, or an animal, come to escort them away."

"An animal?"

"It's an animal with which that person is familiar—a pet, a favorite horse, for example. I once released a man who had been trapped since the end of the eighteenth century, and after I'd been through the catharsis of his death and the things that entrapped him, and he released those emotional energies that were holding him down, I was wondering how he would get away. A large black horse came onto the scene, and he recognized it. It was a horse he loved. He mounted that horse, and the horse trotted out to the courtyard where this scene took place. I was told the horse knows the pastures to which the man belongs."

I asked Eddie to tell me how he had gotten involved in releasement, and what the process is like.

"One of the first events that led me in that direction occurred in the early 1980s when I was at the College of Psychic Studies [in London], and I was talking to Brenda Marshall, then the president, in her office. I said to her that suddenly I was aware that I'd got someone with me who seemed to be deformed in some way. I could feel this man's presence. There was a lot of noise going on outside with pneumatic drills being used close by. The first thing this man said to me was, 'London always was a noisy place, wasn't it?' That was his introduction. I could tell that this man was seriously deformed—it was having an effect on me. You would perhaps call the condition spastic nowadays. It was clear, also, that he was stuck, trapped in the earth plane. I also got this distinct feeling that there was something wrong. And so I tuned further in to him, and he was saying to me, 'I don't want to go where he is, I don't want to go where he is.' He was talking about the cruel master that he had when he was on earth. He was a servant in the Victorian period. This other man had treated him abominably. In fact, the servant said to me that the only relief he got was when he was beaten, as though his life was so terrible that this was an event that somehow put some relief into him. He was afraid that when he died, he would meet up again with this man. He was so terrified that he had fixed himself—he wouldn't let himself move. I had to reassure him that he wouldn't find this man. Once he was reassured, and we'd been through the catharsis of death and the fear that was holding him, these binding energies were released. Somebody came and took him away into the light. Wonderful that was, that experience of being released into the light."

I asked Eddie what he meant by the "catharsis of death."

"The mechanics of the process, as I've come to understand them, are these: that the person being held down by some obsessive aspect of the mind is trapped and can be trapped for a very long period. The first thing one has to do in releasing them is to go through those events which have relevance to this entrapment. Very often it's associated with the death itself. So that means that one has to go through the death with them. I experience the way in which they died. I experience some of the pains that they went through, and I experience also some of the emotional problems that caused them to be stuck. It seems to me that it's rather like the process that people go through under psychiatry, where in order to relieve a neurosis the person is taken back to some event and then taken through the emotions of that event. Once those emotions are released there's subsequently the possibility of cure. It happens much more rapidly with these trapped souls —perhaps five, ten minutes or so before a presence comes onto the scene. This presence may be a relative or friend, and it may occasionally be an animal. There has to be a love connection. That person or animal then escorts the trapped individual onto a pathway which is flooded with light, and takes them to the spiritual levels where they should have gone in the first place had they not been trapped."

"Why can't these escorting beings do the releasing?" I wanted to know. "Why does it have to involve a living person such as yourself?"

"I know I work with a team on the Other Side who cooperate," Eddie said. "They in some way guide the trapped person into my orbit. They then go through the process I've described. That release of energy can be so great that it can cause the soul who is releasing it to, if you like, rebound into psychic space somewhere. My function is as anchor man. I hold a soul steady until that release is effected. The team then comes into play by bringing some person into the scene that the trapped soul recognizes and has confidence in and will accompany. It is team effort, but this business of being anchor man is very, very important. Without it they on the other side would have very much more difficulty rescuing trapped souls."

"Could you explain more about this rebounding?"

"It's difficult to translate it into physical analogy. The impression I get is that when the person releases all this emotional energy that is tied up entrapment, it's like the recoil from a gun. They'll go out of the psychic space that they're in and be more difficult to find. We, being immersed in this material world, are in a good position to prevent that from happening, because we are less easily moved. The power of emotion at this level doesn't have the same effect as it does at the spirit level, where emotion has great power. It is largely a mental realm, and it is ideoplastic—it's a world in which thought can influence action in a very direct way. The release of emotional energy somehow causes the displacement of the person in what corresponds to space to us, but in whatever terms that may be in the next life."

"Why do people become stuck?" I asked.

"The reasons are many indeed. I keep coming across different ones. Perhaps one interesting reason concerned some of the people who died in the earthquake disaster in Armenia several years ago. I became aware that I was contacting people in connection with a disaster, and I wasn't sure what disaster it was. And then I saw the rubble of an earthquake disaster, and I knew: Armenia. I saw a man shepherding a number of people, trying to hold them together, because they were in a state of near panic. I gathered that these people hadn't realized that they'd died, and they were terrified that they would get caught up in another aftershock. They'd taken over with them their terror, and this was the thing that was trapping them. This man seemed to be a natural leader, and he was trying to keep them together.

"I found myself, or part of myself, standing on top of the rubble, looking down on them. I tried to project calm and quiet, but I hadn't any idea how this was going to develop. It's difficult to say how many people there were—perhaps twenty or thirty. It went through my mind that they were going to be very difficult to release from this situation because of their near panic. I thought, 'If some angelic figure comes onto the scene or somebody very bright, there's going to be no holding them.'

"Then an amazing thing happened. I saw a flock of sheep moving onto the scene, toward these people. In Armenia sheep are an everyday thing. But one of the sheep moved toward one of the men, and gently nudged him, and somehow got the man to understand that he should follow him. The man followed the sheep, then the next sheep went to the next person, and so it went on until they'd all been led away. The sheep were leading them, you see, to an area where they would be away from all this rubble and where they would be at peace. They would move on from there to a proper release. But I didn't need to follow it any further. That was it."

"How do you anchor the trapped souls and prevent them from ricocheting into psychic space?"

"I do it mentally—I'm working on a mental level. The mind is so powerful. I was once told, after releasing somebody who'd been trapped for hundreds of years, to observe the power of the mind—how at one extreme it can pin a soul down in time and space, and at the other extreme it can encompass the universe. That just about sums it up. If the mind, which is so powerful in a postmortal condition, if the mind has some obsessive idea, which may be terror or greed, or is fixed on the notion that there is no such thing as survival, then the mind makes sure that the soul is fixed. Won't let it move. I could tell you innumerable stories of this sort of thing. I've got in excess of one hundred fifty cases. They're all different, which makes them very interesting."

"Do you have any idea how many souls are trapped?" I wondered.

"It's a small minority of people, that's for sure, but it is still a significant number. The chance of one getting trapped, I would guess, is less than one in several hundred. But the entrapment can persist for a long time. I have come across cases where people have been trapped for hundreds of years."

"Do any earthbound souls attach themselves to living people and cause problems?"

"Sometimes, but usually not," Eddie said. "I've recently come across one or two cases where mothers have been possessively attached to their daughters. That can cause a lot of unpleasantness, and it's a big relief to the daughter once the mother is escorted away. But it's not a forced release—none of it is forced. The souls concerned have to begin to understand that they're in the wrong place. Once they understand that, they can move on.

"One of the most remarkable cases I've come across like that was at the College of Psychic Studies where I happened to be one day. I don't go there very often. The president, Brenda Marshall, asked me to see a lady who'd just come in, with a pain in her head or neck. She'd been carrying this pain around for the last seven years, and she'd been in countries all over the world seeking relief. She'd also been on morphine, but nothing did anything for it. So I met the lady, and we went into one of the rooms, and I started to talk to her and tune in to her. I became aware that there was a presence with her. I described this presence, and she recognized it as a man, a Mexican whom she'd nursed through terminal cancer. He died of a tumor on the brain. This presence became very strong, and then I made contact with him. I went through his death experience with him and released him from entrapment. It seemed that as the tumor developed he went into a coma. He was forced out of his body and saw it lying on the bed. He could neither get into it nor get away from it, because the body was still alive. He became very, very frustrated. When he died, he attached himself to this lady, because, as he said to me, when he went away from her he went into a darkness. In this attachment he was transferring to her the still very vivid memory of all the pain that he went through, and she was experiencing his pain. He apologized for having caused her this pain. Then it was possible to get help for him. The team on the other side, whoever they are, took him away. Her pain went immediately. I realized her aura or etheric body was damaged because of his attachment. I worked for some time, about twenty minutes, doing my best to seal off her aura. I walked out and left her to sit quietly on her own. A few minutes later she came out, rushing round the college saying, 'He's done a miracle, he's done a miracle!'

"I had a case involving a lady who felt uneasy about her mother, who had passed over. I quickly found the mother, and I saw a room that looked like a kitchen. In front of the fireplace there was a trap door. Just as I came onto the scene, somebody had gone down through the trap door and was about to slam the door down. It was the mother. Didn't want me to find her. I said to the daughter, 'It's no good me trying to pursue her down there. She doesn't want to be found, and I can't find her if she doesn't want to be found. We'll have to leave her for a bit and hope that something can be done in the meantime.'

"I came back to the scene the next day. This time I was able to make contact with the mother. She had been watching her daughter's actions, or as much as she could perceive of them through a little window in the kitchen wall. This window, I could see, was about eight inches wide by about fourteen tall. It looked like smoked glass. Whenever she wanted to make contact with her daughter, which was most of the time, she would be peering through this little window. It reminded me of what St. Paul felt, seen through a glass darkly.

"This illustrates something that I've found time and time again—that at this other, postmortem level, what we would regard as allegorical becomes real. It's important, I think, that I keep coming across this. The mother was seeing her daughter through this allegorical window, but it was a real window to her. Through this she was interfering a lot with her daughter. She was influencing her, and her mind would be reaching out toward her daughter, trying to control her. It was a very nasty situation.

"When I found the mother, I had to persuade her to step into a circle of light that had appeared before her. It took some time to persuade her to do this. She stood and eventually she made the step. Once she stepped into it, the background of the kitchen faded away. That was no longer relevant. I suppose it was a change of vibration. She was escorted away, and I knew she had a journey to make. In a case where somebody has been causing mischief, they don't go straight to the spirit world at the level that most people enter. They have a journey to make, and it's an upward journey that has many allegorical aspects in it. They find obstructions, and they've got to get past them—they can't dodge them. Each one represents some psychological or moral aspect of what they've got to overcome on this journey. They're invariably escorted, sometimes invisibly, sometimes visibly by somebody, and sometimes even by an animal."

"A beloved animal again?"

"This whole business of the part played by animals is intriguing," Eddie said. "I've found animals playing all sorts of roles. Love is always a part of it. I came across a man who had committed suicide and who was trapped as a result. People tend go into limbo when they commit suicide, and they don't get released. It's reckoned that as a rule they don't get released until the end of what would have been their natural life. They don't appreciate the passage of time while they're in that condition. Unfortunately, whatever problems caused them to commit suicide tend to keep recycling for them all the time. They don't get away from them. It's a terrible, terrible existence. However, if people commit suicide under circumstances where they haven't the responsibility for their actions, it's a way different story.

"When I found this man trapped by suicide, I discovered something important—that we can intercede, that our prayerful thoughts for them can result in an amelioration of their condition. That's why it's so important to pray for those who committed suicide and to send them love. It's very precious to them in their condition, very precious.

"This man was feeling his loneliness. It was a terrible loneliness. I asked for help for him. A little dog appeared. I knew that little dog would stay with him through the period of entrapment. To that man, it was a great help.

"I also came across a man who had committed suicide by gassing himself with exhaust in the back of a small van. I was asked to look into this on behalf of his family, who wanted to know where he was and what had happened to him after death. When I picked him up he was lying in a small box on his elbow, propped up in the attitude that he was in when he died. I couldn't make out what this small box was. It was only later I discovered that he had gassed himself in the back of a small van, and that's what I was seeing. His mental picture of where he was, was the same. The thought of him being stuck there many years, until his life would have expired naturally, was so awful. I asked if something could be done for him. After a time he was lifted out of this van in a most remarkable way. He was just levitated out of this van into the light, and he was put into a little grotto. Now, he was still confined, and he wouldn't be able to move outside that little grotto, but it was a tremendous improvement on where he had been. This is the sort of thing we can do to help. I don't think we need to be psychic to do this. I think if we know somebody who has committed suicide, and we ask that their lot be ameliorated as much as possible, then these sorts of things will happen."

Eddie had another case that illustrated the impact of mortal emotions on the postmortem state.

"I suddenly became aware of contact with a woman, and that she was in great distress. I tuned in and I began to see her. She was dressed in Victorian costume. I got the impression of the late nineteenth century. She was wheeling a market barrow.

"She started to say, 'I cared for them, I looked after them, and they didn't bother with me when I grew old.' I gathered that she was terribly upset because she'd brought up quite a large family, and worked very hard in the market with her husband. When her husband died she still carried on. She brought the children up. When they were grown up, she felt they didn't help her enough. She was having to go on working in the market with this heavy barrow, taking the goods there, and selling them and wheeling it back again in order to earn enough money to keep herself alive. She became embittered about this. Understandable, in a way.

"This was what had trapped her, so I went through all this with her. Still, she seemed to have something that hadn't revealed itself. Then it began to show. I could see her standing in this cobbled street—this was the cobbled street of her memory, if you like. It was her mental construct that she was in. She said, 'God shouldn't have let it happen, God shouldn't have let it happen.' She began to rail against God. She grew more and more angry as she released this. Then she started to run. She ran along this cobbled road and tripped over her own skirts, fell headlong. She was beating the ground with her fists as she lay there, and shouting and in a terrible state of distress, and so very angry with God. Once she'd finished expressing all this anger, she got up, and after a time she was escorted away into the light.

"I could see that what had entrapped her were her feelings of deep religious guilt that she was blaming God for her situation. She couldn't come face to face with that. She felt unworthy because she was blaming God. She was a very difficult case. When she was escorted away, I thought to myself, that's good, she's gone. A voice said to me, 'What are you going to do about the anger?' I puzzled about this.

"Then I saw what appeared to be a globe of glass or plastic, or a bubble, huge, about three or four feet across, poised three or four feet above the ground where this cobbled road was. Inside it were flames and a great deal of activity. A very menacing-looking thing. 'What are you going to do about that?' the voice asked. I said, 'What *can* I do about it?' The voice said, 'You've got to dissolve it with love.'

"I projected love around this object as it was hovering. Gradually it got smaller and smaller and smaller until it vanished. Then I was told, 'If you'd not done this, this would have drifted about and then caused a great deal of harm if it had touched someone either at the earth level or the next level.'"

Eddie had a glimpse of an angel in one healing. "I started to do healing with the lady who'd learned she'd got cancer, and had the hysterectomy. When I went to see her, while I was talking to her, I realized that there would be an angelic presence with her when she went in for this operation. I asked her to visualize this, and to try and draw it closer to her. This I did on other occasions with people who were going in for operations involving general anesthetic. I felt there was always an angelic presence going with them. Once I saw this angelic presence, but not fully. I saw the edge of a garment, and it was a brilliant white. And I knew that I wasn't seeing the whole of this figure, because it would have been too blinding. I came to progressively understand how important it was for people, if they could, to understand that an angel was present. I think the reason for the angel being present, particularly in operations where there is a general anesthetic, is that the operation is like a near death. The soul is moved out of the body and therefore has to be protected so that nothing else can gain entry. Just as there is an angel present at death, so this angel is present during operations. I used to call this the Angel of Operations. I couldn't think of any other word for it.

"I made a point when I knew somebody was going to have an operation of always invoking this angel. It would always be there, but I think if the person undergoing the operation could be made to understand that it was there, then the presence could be drawn closer and a lot of help would come out of it. This has been people's experience—in a number of cases they've felt that there was a presence with them. I think angels are present in other circumstances of importance—for example, at birth. I'm sure that they play a major part in that process, and in the processes from conception right up to birth. I believe that there is a hierarchy of angels just as there is a hierarchy of most spirit entities. There is a level in the angelic kingdom where angels overlook houses. I sometimes wonder if, when a house becomes empty, the reason it falls into decay is as much because the angel withdraws as because of physical decay. A house that's been empty for a long time has a great sadness about it. It's got something lacking. We think the thing it's lacking is that it's got nobody living in it. But I think it goes beyond that. The house has ceased to function in the way that a life has function."

Eddie went on, "I've had one stunning experience in relation to angels. This was a case where an angelic being elected to come into the human race. It happens rarely. A lady I knew several years ago was very concerned about her grandson. He was a highly intelligent boy. She is psychic and was aware that he was in touch with the darker psychic side on the astral level. Yet, surprisingly, he seemed to be in control. This was very puzzling. In fact, in terms of normal human experience, he was taking awful risks, and he was virtually playing games with certain entities on that level. He also seemed to be getting himself into all sorts of mischief, including scrapes with the police. He was behaving in such a way that she was concerned he'd end up in prison. One night I woke up and I was told that this young man, who was about sixteen, was an angelic being who'd elected to come back into the human race. In doing this, he brought with him some remembrance of his former powers at an unconscious level. It was this remembrance that was leading him into the sort of adventures he was having with the dark side, in which he seemed, surprisingly, to be able to control events. I was also told that at a deeper level he was anxious to get as much experience as fast as possible in the human situation. This was leading him into the sort of behavior that we would regard as very chancy.

"I told the grandmother that I thought it was possible that he would go on getting himself into trouble. That he might even foreshorten his life through an accident or some such, in order to come back after a fairly short interval to learn more in different circumstances. It was as though this being that was projecting as this boy had a need to learn as much as possible as quickly as possible. When we looked at his behavior in the light of this, and what she already knew about him, it did account for the things that were puzzling her, and she accepted this. It helped her in one way that she could see that there was a reason and a logic behind the way he was behaving.

"What happened to him?" I asked.

"He continued to get himself into trouble, and the last time I heard about him, he was up for several court cases."

"Why would an angel elect to come into the human race?"

"I think the angelic kingdom is trusted with much power because it's incorruptible," Eddie answered. "This is why God uses the angels as his messengers. The same power could not be given to human beings because they couldn't be trusted with it. They are so corruptible. The angelic kingdom watches the human kingdom, and is very—it's difficult to find quite the right word—is very interested, almost envious of the way that the human race can advance spiritually through suffering. The angelic kingdom is unable to do this. It doesn't find itself in the sorts of situations that the human kingdom does."

"How do angels advance then?"

"They have to advance through service. The reason an angel occasionally elects to come into the human race is that this particular entity is willing to sacrifice its peculiar advantages as an angel in order to advance virtually in the same way that the human being can advance. It is possible that such a being will connect to and revert back into the angelic kingdom at some point in the distant future."

"Does that mean that angels have souls?"

"The angels are eternal beings. They show themselves ordinarily in a form that we can recognize, but, in fact, they are creatures beyond body. They show themselves in ways that we imagine they should look like. Much the same as the fairy kingdom shows itself in ways that we can recognize. But they are, at least on the higher levels, far beyond the need for form."

"Do you think angels are assigned roles or functions?"

"There are angels with all sorts of functions," Eddie answered. "There are angels who are concerned with landscape and with looking after people and guarding homes, or at least overlighting homes in a spiritual sense. There are angels who have a degree of spiritual responsibility toward nations, and others who have a degree of responsibility toward the clearest aspects of the planet earth. These functions are, to some degree, in parallel with those of the devic kingdom. The devic kingdom is in a relationship to the angelic kingdom that is like the relationship we have with the angelic and devic kingdoms. They are parallel, cooperating beings, and all are progressing upward."

"Toward what?" I asked.

"Toward God, toward greater wisdom and understanding of God's ultimate purpose. We know that we are, in this life and in the many lives that we have, gathering together experience both of good and evil, and that we are taking this experience with us and joining into groups, and that we garner out of this experience the aspects which will carry us forward to higher and higher levels. We start as pure and innocent spirits and have to fall, as Adam and Eve fell, and then work our way steadily upward. In the process we've lost the innocence, but we've gathered wisdom."

"If angels can advance through service, why would they want to do it through suffering?"

"Suffering brings about a different sort and faster rate of development," Eddie responded.

"Do you have any idea how many angels might be walking among us for various reasons?"

"No. I've learned more and more not to discount anything. I was once told that we set limits on our capabilities and our understandings through our imagination. If only we were to set free our imagination in a constructive way, we could advance more in the spiritual and psychic realms. Always around us, in the mental field, there is a horizon which we ourselves set. We push it back every now and again, but we would make faster progress in some directions if we were to free our imagination in a constructive way."

"Why is it important for us human beings to become closer to the angel realm, and how is it possible?"

"First of all, it is God's purpose that we do cooperate with the angelic kingdom. I think that the angelic kingdom has been waiting a very long time for the opportunity for us to recognize their existence. The angelic kingdom has fallen out of recognition with most people in the Western world, who relegate the whole idea to the Old Testament and the stories there, and think that angel stories don't happen anymore. We think that the angelic kingdom, if it ever existed, served their purpose with God in the Old Testament times. In this way, the angelic kingdom has had to stand aside for most people, sadly waiting for human beings to come round to the realization that many of the problems that have beset us, and particularly those that beset us now in regard to the planet, can only be solved by recognizing their existence and cooperating with them. They have the power, the understanding to help us in ways that we are powerless to work. It's absolutely vital that we recognize this."

"And how can we reach out to them?"

"By transferring the notion of the angelic kingdom at the mind or intellectual level down to the heart level, so it becomes a deep conviction. We must work on that conviction. The more the imagination opens constructively to recognize that there is this possibility, then the closer we shall become to angels and the faster we shall be able to transfer what is an intellectual understanding at best into this deeper, heartfelt conviction. When we reach that heart level, then cooperation can become real, and we shall begin to have an inner knowing and an inner understanding of the angelic purpose. After all, the power they harness could be used—and should be used—in solving our problems."

Eddie continued, "Angels have a special relationship between us and the devic kingdom. The devic kingdom has a somewhat narrower horizon, with duties of or relating to all natural events, and all those things which are necessary to try and put the earth to rights. But the angelic kingdom has access to powers of a different sort from that of the devic kingdom. The devic kingdom has immense powers that would dwarf anything that man has ever been able to achieve in the way of power. Of that I am certain, because I've had some contact with that. The angelic kingdom has a different quality of power, a more spiritual power. The spiritual power is somehow mediated, so that it can be used in cooperation with the devic power. Here again, the human race has a vital part to play. Then we shall begin to reverse the sort of harm that we've done to the earth."

"How have you experienced the devic kingdom?"

"A number of times I've had the devic approach made to me by devas of the air, devas that control wind and storms and so on. The feeling that they give is not the same as the feeling one gets from spiritual entities or human spiritual entities. It is a degree of detachment. There is the feeling that the devic kingdom, in following the pathway of action that is set for it, is quite prepared to wreak destruction at the human level. It doesn't want to, but it is prepared to do so if that is what is necessary. The devic kingdom stands aside to some degree. It does offer us cooperation, it does ask us to respect it. But if we don't, then it's quite capable of bringing about such forces that can cause great damage.

"I think if we continue to damage the earth, we should bring about the results that are being caused by our action. In manifesting these results, the devic kingdom would be immediately affected. They wouldn't react in any vengeful way. They have indicated that they are capable of withdrawing their cooperation in matters like crop growth, and if we continue to break the spiritual laws that we should be obeying, they might do so. Again, it's not revenge, it's simply that they would have to withdraw cooperation because cooperation with us would be impossible."

"Do we give the devas a form the same way we give angels a form?" I asked.

"I've never seen a deva. But they seem to be able, without any difficulty at all, to communicate intelligently to us, and invariably bring with them a certain degree of detachment, and also an immense, awesome power, especially those that relate to the physical kingdom as distinct from the plant kingdom. This awesome power is very restrained. Quite clearly their primary interest is not us at all. Their primary interest is in making the physical kingdom and the plant kingdom and the rest of nature operate as it's supposed to operate."

"Do we all have guardian angels?"

"Yes. I think there's a level of the angelic kingdom which on a one-to-one basis looks after us quite apart from the spirit guides that we are sometimes told about. Again, this is cooperation. There's a power of cooperation at many levels. Each one of the units, or each one of the separate lines that we've been talking about, seems to have its own function, and they operate cooperatively, which brings us back to the whole thing about the angelic kingdom. We're trying to operate ignoring it, overlooking it, not even believing in it. We're quite prepared to think about the spirit kingdom, but humans haven't extended their ideas beyond that. What we've got to do is to recognize that there are these three kingdoms and probably others. The human spiritual kingdom, the angelic kingdom, and the devic kingdom have all got their part to play, and in their various functioning they all need each other."

I wondered if animals have angels that look over them.

"They certainly have devic protectors," Eddie said. "Each species has a devic spirit which guards it, guides it, and is responsible for its future development."

Eddie said that he did not believe that the angelic kingdom directly intervenes at the physical level. "Instead, they bring powers to bear which both the human and devic kingdoms can use."

After spending two fascinating days with Eddie learning about his work, I asked him if he could contact the angel realm for me. "I'd like to ask them for their advice concerning my research," I said.

Eddie agreed, though he pointed out that he had never before attempted to contact directly the angel realm, primarily because of the intensity of the energy there. He was uncertain that his human consciousness could access such brilliance, but he would give it a try. The session turned out to be one of the most incredible I've ever experienced with a medium.

We got comfortable in the sitting room at Inlight House. The room had been warmed with heaters and a fire, and Eddie turned the heat back. I sat in the chintz sofa, notebook and pen ready to take down dictation. Eddie sat opposite me in a straight-backed chair.

Eddie closed his eyes and began the process of elevating his consciousness. I closed my eyes and relaxed, soaking up the pleasant atmosphere that saturated the house.

After some time—I was not sure how many minutes had passed—I was suddenly aware of a presence in the room. I opened my eyes but could see nothing out of the ordinary. Yet a presence was there, so powerful and intense that it created a pressure in the room, as though we were plunged underwater. I had the feeling that the presence was a light beyond the ability of the human eye to perceive. In addition, I felt the room become hot, even though the heat was turned down.

The pressure and heat built in intensity. Then Eddie, eyes closed, began to speak. I was able to focus on what he was saying and write it down. The session lasted but a few minutes, and the pressure continued to build until it became almost painful. Yet it was a pleasant pain, if that makes any sense. I can perhaps compare it only to the ecstatic pain experienced by some mystics.

The message delivered was this:

"Your interest in the angelic kingdom is purposeful, the full import of which will only be revealed in the course of time. You are being used by the angelic kingdom as a willing and valuable servant to help bring about a greater awareness of the angelic function. Be prepared at some stage to be lifted in your inner vision. What you see will tax your powers of description. This will be presented to you by those angels working most closely with you. You are not yet ready for this illumination. We call upon you to tune in to this kingdom not by act of will but by dedication likened to sanctified purpose. Our kingdom is one of great light, and few humans are fit to view it. You will be given the necessary protection.

"As for your work, rest assured that we take sufficient measure according to our purpose. Remember this also: do not reduce us in any way to suit humanity's understanding. This would not be right. Raise humanity instead to meet us through inspired understanding. Impress on people that we are not as they. We are not human. We are no closer to God than you are. But we serve his purpose in a way that you would judge to be more direct. We express a power that you would not understand as yet, except if you experience it. The word you would choose would be 'ineffable.'

"We differ from you in a number of essential ways. We have no pride. But we have much love. We bear the very essence of unconditional love. Yet we have the power to direct this and place it where God would have us do so. We seek earnestly to raise the human understanding, to bring it to a sufficient level where the answers to pressing problems can be found. We shall not give the answers—that is not our function. These will come from the devic kingdom working closely with those inspired in the human kingdom.

"So, do you see our function more clearly? In your writing, check what you say against what has been given here, and you will do us a great service, and in turn, humanity. Our blessings come to you now, shafted in intense light, which would not be fitting for you to see, but which will lift you and inspire you in the work ahead. We say farewell with the thought that you and we are likewise children of God doing his purpose."

As the message was finished, the pressure in the room began to dissipate. I didn't want the presence to leave. Don't go! I thought, but the presence continued to withdraw. I asked if I could pose questions. The angels responded through Eddie, "Yes."

I had never asked questions of angels in this manner before, and for a few moments, I was stymied. Frankly, I was torn between personal matters and cosmic matters. As if they read my thoughts, the angels admonished, "Do not trivialize."

So, there would be no lowly fortune-telling from the angel kingdom. Of course!

I decided to ask what had puzzled me for years. "Who is Silver Lady?"

There was a moment of silence, and then Silver Lady herself came on the scene to answer. "You do not have quite an accurate picture of me," she said. "I am not an angel but am of the angel realm and of the human realm. My function is to be intermediate between the angel kingdom and the human kingdom for the purpose of interpretation. Seek not to identify me more closely at this stage."

And with that, Eddie could no longer physically sustain his effort, and the connection was broken.

After a session, Eddie does a visualization to close down his chakras. But the intensity of the angel kingdom was so great that he found himself unable to shut down his psychic centers himself. He was in obvious discomfort, shaky, red in the face, with trickles of sweat running down his cheeks. He asked me if I had ever done any healing, and I said that I'd had training in therapeutic touch. He directed me to place my hands over his shoulder blades. I did so, and felt like I'd placed my hands inches over a radiator. Heat was pouring from his body. I made smoothing motions in his aura, which he said would help his pituitary gland. After several minutes he felt all right.

We discussed the session. Eddie said that as he had begun his meditation to send his consciousness to the angel realm, he had felt a being—some sort of helping spirit—come between him and the angels. This measure was protective, intended to decrease the intense angelic energy, which otherwise would have overwhelmed Eddie's consciousness. The being remained in place throughout the reading. I thought that some sort of buffer had protected me as well, making me aware of light that was beyond my ability to see it, without adversely affecting my senses.

I was particularly struck by the angels' statement that they are no closer to God than are humans but just tread a different path. That contradicts what has been handed down to us by philosophers and church authorities. Yet it made sense to me.

As for Silver Lady, we were both surprised by her description of herself, which indicated that she might be half human, half angel—a sort of hybrid we'd never before contemplated. We wondered how many other hybrids there might be, and where they existed in relation to the angel realm. I also was puzzled about why I'd been admonished not to inquire more into her identity or nature. And I was anxious to have the uplifting the angels described. However, nearly two years would elapse before that occurred.

Since then, when I've described the session to others, I've been asked why the angels did not define themselves in terms of "What is an angel?" In fact, they did, by describing their function and nature. But angels are beyond definition in the human sense, and we waste a lot of time looking at trees and missing the forest. Instead of being preoccupied with what angels "are" and look like, we should focus on their essence: unconditional love.

But let's return to England, for there was more with Eddie.

The session with the angels would have been wonderful enough, but it was my last night in England on this particular trip, and so Eddie graciously agreed to contact the deva realm as well. I was curious to see what they might say about crop circles, those mysterious formations impressed by unknown means into grain crops in England and elsewhere in the world. I had been researching crop circles, and had just established the Center for North American Crop Circle Studies as a nonprofit organization to advance study of the phenomenon.

First, we relaxed and regained our energy by going for a long walk in the beautiful woods around Inlight House. It was late fall, and most of the trees were bare. We then walked a trail into the village of Grayshott, where we had tea and cakes. After supper back at Inlight House, we returned to the sitting room for another session.

The deva session was very different from the angel session. As Eddie shifted his consciousness, the heat in the room rose, as it had during the angel session. And, as in the angel session, I felt an intensity, a pressure in the room, only of a much different sort. It was not light-beyond-human-ability-to-see. Instead, the energy seemed to well up from the earth, and seemed to be outside the house as well as in it. I could feel it mostly as a pressure against my sinuses and chest. It was a primal energy, raw and hard, the energy of tempests and hurricanes and tornadoes. This energy was controlled by the devas who answered our call. I felt that this energy could easily be turned against us in a destructive way if the devas were so instructed. The wind, which had been still throughout the day and early evening, began to blow harder and harder and to whip around the house in an eerie scream.

To reach the devas, Eddie first made contact with the spirit of a Native American, who offered to perform the dance that would summon the beings we sought. As the spirit danced, Eddie tapped out the rhythm with his hands. Then the message came:

"Those of my race knew of the devic kingdom. We could call them up when we needed special help. There was a special rhythm—a drum rhythm—and a dance for each one. For the spirit of the trees, for the spirit of the sky, and of the wind, and of the rain, and the rivers, and the plains, and the mountains. Our lives were intimately woven into the fabric of nature and the supernatural beings who governed all these aspects.

"You wish to make contact with the devic kingdom. I will dance for you. And beat out the rhythm with my feet to call up my brother, the spirit of the land. He is one with whom you need to get better acquainted. It would help if you made the room quiet."

I got up and turned off the stereo, which was playing a Gregorian chant. At this point, I could hear the wind come up outside. After I resumed my seat, there were a few moments of silence, and then Eddie began to speak again, this time in a voice distinctly different from that of the Native American spirit.

"When will you learn? We watch and wait. And feel the pain as you destroy our kingdom. Time is running out. The land you desecrate will lose its fertility. And the rain which is our friend shall wash away the soil, and the wind shall blow away the dust. And the dust shall settle on the upturned faces of those who would not learn.

"This need not happen. But time is running out. We see encouraging signs here and there. A small awakening. But it must take hold.

"You seek to tell of the reality of the angelic world. This is good. But you will make their task and ours and your own far more difficult unless you take heed. If it is a close-run thing [pushing the limits of time], many will suffer and there will be despair. We can do certain things which lie within our power. But the many people that dwell on the earth must seek assistance from the source higher than themselves.

"If the effort to do this manifests, we will be able to

cooperate. We know already that humanity has a high price to pay for its foolishness. I am telling you what some are slowly coming to know. You must bend all your efforts in prayer to God to help you make the contacts that are essential if you are to turn the tide. We do the will of the Creator. We do not do man's will. In his ignorance he undoes much of our work. Why is he so blind?"

At the time, I did not feel as illuminated by the devas' message, as powerful as it was, as I had by the angels' message. I wanted answers to the crop circles, and they had given none. Of course, the answers cannot be handed to us; we must discover them for ourselves, within our own consciousness. Crop circles are consciousness expanders, forcing us to look within for connection to all things and the divine.

In both sessions, I did not necessarily get the information I sought. Instead, I got the information I needed, which is always the case when humanity turns to higher sources for help.

════ **9** ════

Healing Helpers

If angels make themselves available to help human-kind, then surely one of their most important tasks is to heal. There are different kinds of healing—physical, emotional, spiritual. When we are faced with catastrophic or terminal illness, or permanent injuries, sometimes we cannot be cured physically, but we can be healed spiritually. Many persons who work in medicine and health care have had strange experiences that are both wonderful and eerie, in which presences and energies from beyond the physical plane manifest to help the patient. In particular, persons who work in alternative healing, including lay healers such as Eddie Burks who work through laying on of hands or energy transfers, are often acutely aware of presences that guide them in their work. Some call these presences God or Jesus; some call them angels.

The healing ministry of angels is established in

Tobit, one of the books of the Apocrypha. Tobit tells how the angel Raphael, whose name means "the shining one who heals," provides magical formulae for healing. The story underscores the concept that angels do not act on their own but are emissaries of God, and that they have no physical form but can create the appearance of form for the benefit of humans.

The story concerns a pious man named Tobit and his son, Tobias. It takes place in the late eighth-century B.C. in the Assyrian capital of Nineveh, where the people of northern Israel have been taken captive. The storyteller is Tobit himself, who is instructed by Raphael to write an account of the events that happen to him, his son, and others.

By his own description, Tobit was a model of piety, walking "in the ways of truth and righteousness." He gave money, food, and clothing to the poor. He defied Sennacherib the king by burying his fellow Israeli dead, whose bodies had been left in the open by their captors.

On one occasion Tobit, who was fifty years old, was just sitting down to dinner when he learned of another corpse that needed burying. He left his meal and attended to the body. He was defiled from handling the corpse and so did not return home that night but slept by the wall of the courtyard. He left his face uncovered.

Unknown to Tobit, sparrows were perched on the wall, and their droppings fell into his eyes, rendering him blind. He sought the help of various physicians, to no avail. His wife was forced to work to earn money.

After eight years, Tobit, depressed and in despair,

begged God to let him die. In preparation for death, he called in his only son and told him to journey to Media, where he had left some money in trust with another man. He instructed Tobias to find a man to accompany him on the journey, and he would pay the man's wages for his time and trouble.

While this drama was unfolding in Nineveh, another was taking place in Media, where a young woman named Sarah was possessed by the demon Asmodeus, "the destroyer." Sarah had been given to seven men in wedlock, but the demon had killed them all on their wedding night, before the marriages could be consummated. Sarah's parents, Raguel and Edna, feared they would never marry off their only daughter.

God heard the prayers of both Tobit and Raguel and dispatched Raphael to heal Tobit's blindness and exorcise the demon from Sarah.

When Tobias went looking for a man to accompany him on the trip to Media, he found Raphael, who appeared as a human and introduced himself as Azarius, the son of one of Tobit's relatives. They struck a deal for wages and departed.

The first evening they camped along the Tigris River. Tobias went down to the river to wash, and a giant fish jumped up and threatened to swallow him. Raphael told him to catch it, which he did with his hands, and threw it up on the bank. Raphael said, "Cut open the fish and take the heart and liver and gall and put them away safely." Tobias did this. They then roasted and ate the rest of the fish.

Tobias asked the angel what use were the saved parts.

Raphael replied, "As for the heart and the liver, if a demon or evil spirit gives trouble to anyone, you make a smoke from these before the man or woman, and that person will never be troubled again. And as for the gall, anoint with it a man who has white films in his eyes, and he will be cured."

As they neared their destination, Raphael told Tobias that they would stay in the house of Raguel, and that he should take Sarah as his wife. Understandably, Tobias was not thrilled to learn that seven prospective husbands had all died at the hands of the demon. But the angel assured him, "When you enter the bridal chamber, you shall take live ashes of incense and lay upon them some of the heart and liver of the fish so as to make a smoke. Then the demon will smell it and flee away, and will never again return. And when you approach her, rise up, both of you, and cry out to the merciful God, and he will save you and have mercy on you. Do not be afraid, for she was destined for you from eternity. You will save her, and she will go with you, and I suppose you will have children by her."

The events came to pass as the angel predicted. Tobias was offered the hand of Sarah in marriage, and a contract was drawn up immediately. In the bridal chamber, Tobias followed Raphael's instructions for exorcising Asmodeus. The demon fled to "the remotest parts of Egypt" (the traditional home of magic and witchcraft), where Raphael bound him up.

After a fourteen-day wedding feast, Tobias, his bride, and Raphael returned home to Tobit. Tobias anointed his father's eyes with the gall of the fish, and Tobit's sight was restored. In gratitude, he and Tobias offered Raphael half of the monies that Tobias had retrieved from Media.

The angel then revealed his true self to the men. "I

am Raphael, one of the seven holy angels who present the prayers of the saints and enter in the presence of the glory of the Holy One," he said. He told Tobit that he had been ever present with him, and had taken his prayers for healing to God. He urged the men to praise and thank God, and to lead righteous lives.

Tobit and Tobias were alarmed to be in the presence of an archangel, and fell to the ground in fear. But Raphael assured them no harm would befall them. "For I did not come as a favor on my part, but by the will of our God," he said. "Therefore praise him forever. All these days I merely appeared to you and did not eat or drink, but you were seeing a vision. And now give thanks to God, for I am ascending to him who sent me. Write in a book everything that has happened." And with that, Raphael vanished.

Raphael continues to minister to healing needs, taking the earnest prayers of humans to God, and responding when assigned. Perhaps he is assisted by a host of other healing angels as well, for those who work as healers attest to a variety of helping angelic beings. Are they other angels, working under Raphael's supervision? Or are they Raphael himself, manifesting in whatever guises are required?

Rosemary's Angels

Rosemary Gardner Loveday, whom we met in chapter 4, is a talented English clairvoyant, medium, and healer, who radiates a gentle angelic energy. She has been clairvoyant from childhood—a gift passed down through the family on her mother's side—and has been cognizant of angels and souls of the dead for most of her life. For Rosemary, the boundaries between our physical world and other realms are often thin or transparent. From these other realms come divine guidance that provide her with extraordinary gifts. Her work has gained her increasing attention on both sides of the Atlantic. She has helped many people in their struggles with physical illness and other difficulties in life. People often report that her very presence is soothing and healing. When they compliment her on the beneficial effects of a reading or healing, she demurs, saying, "It is God working through the angels."

I met Rosemary in 1991, during a trip to England. We were introduced by a mutual friend, Graham Wyley, one of England's leading ghost investigators. I don't believe in coincidences, so I can say that surely the angels orchestrated the event.

I'd taken the train down to Exeter, in Devon, to appear on BBC Radio Devon with Graham. My itinerary called for heading further south to Torquay, where I'd made arrangements to interview a family about a haunting. At the BBC station, I learned that the family had to cancel, so I was left with a free day and evening before having to return to London. After the radio show, I talked with Graham about my angel research and also shared some difficulties I was experiencing in my personal life.

"I know just the person you need to see," he said, explaining to me Rosemary's talents. "But she's very busy, and I don't know if I can get you an appointment tonight."

He called Rosemary and learned that a client had canceled an appointment that evening. I was booked.

At the time, Rosemary lived in the little fishing village of Brixham, tucked onto a cliff on one side of

Tor Bay, looking out to palmy Torquay—the "English Riviera"—on the other side. Graham and his wife, Thelma, also lived in Brixham at the time. (Since then, Rosemary has relocated to Kent, and the Wyleys have moved to Hertsfordshire.)

Later that evening, Graham and Thelma dropped me off at Rosemary's home, Lobster Pot Cottage. I was greeted by a tall woman with a serene and beatific presence and a soft, angelic voice. I relaxed and knew that I was in good hands.

Rosemary escorted me into the cottage. It was warm and inviting. Built in 1640, it featured three small rooms downstairs: a sitting room with fireplace, a dining room, and a kitchen. The low ceilings had exposed beams. There was an atmosphere of peace and tranquility, which seemed to be the product of Rosemary herself.

Rosemary fixed me a cup of tea, and we sat down at a little wooden table in the dining room. I handed her my watch, and she proceeded to give me a reading.

Over the years, I had been to many psychics, mediums, and channelers, and seldom did I receive what I considered to be a good reading. Eddie Burks was the notable exception. Essentially I believe that we can get our answers ourselves, by developing our intuition and tuning ourselves to the inner voice, which delivers information from a higher source. Readings by others can be helpful, however, when we are too close to problems to see the forest for the trees, or when we need an extra stimulus to take action or confront a situation.

The reading that Rosemary gave me was remarkable. It was accurate, but accuracy alone only validates the facts. More important, her reading was permeated with a sensitivity that was as though she truly were seeing things from my eyes. It gave me lots of new insights, and I felt much better.

After the reading, Rosemary gave me healing. She said a silent prayer for guidance and then placed her hands on me where directed to do so. I felt surrounded by invisible but loving presences, and heat and energy flowed into me, as if I were a battery being recharged. Rosemary told me later that during the healing she had a vision of a meter, like a gas-tank gauge, rising from empty to full. It certainly expressed my own feelings of having been refreshed and restored.

Rosemary and I became good friends and have since visited each other whenever we've had the chance. On one occasion I had what I considered an unusual healing of illness from her.

It took place in January, when the weather was cold and damp. I arrived in Brixham feeling a severe respiratory infection seizing hold of me. I was badly congested in my head and chest and feared that my entire stay with Rosemary was going to consist of lying in a sickbed.

Rosemary offered to give me healing. I agreed, though I doubted that anything would help. Sure, it might give me an infusion of energy, but cure me of a cold or bronchitis? I've had countless respiratory infections in my life and recognize the signs of being beyond staving it off—after symptoms are advanced to a certain point, I just have to ride it out for several days.

After making her prayer for divine guidance, Rosemary placed her hands on my head and then at the base of my throat. These positions were held until she received guidance to cease. Then she took me into the sitting room, where a fire crackled in the fireplace, and tucked me onto the sofa with instructions to take a nap. When I woke up two hours later, most of my congestion was gone, and I was well by the next day. I was amazed. It was the first time I'd ever been cured of something by a laying on of hands.

A cold is one thing, and major illness is another. Rosemary has aided people with serious disorders. I hasten to add that she does not diagnose, nor does she advocate alternative healing as a replacement for standard medical treatment. The people who come to see her are guided, she believes, by angelic hands, and they seek her kind of healing in addition to other treatments. Perhaps most of all, they seek the angelic comfort that emanates through her.

Rosemary feels the constant presence of angels in her readings and healings, and also the ongoing presence of her own guardian angel, as we saw in chapter 4. "When I'm doing my healing, I feel angels draw close," Rosemary said. "They help me with my healing. I'm just a channel. They draw close to give people peace. Peace and love come foremost from God, but he sends angels out to gather around people. I handed my life over to God to help heal people. I think if you hand your life over to be used in that way, he's going to send you help."

Rosemary's perception of angels dates to her early childhood, spent in Suffolk, Essex, and Hampshire. Like her mother and grandmother, she saw angels and the dead and had premonitions and intuitions about things that were going to happen. When she talked about these experiences to others, she got puzzling or negative reactions, indicating that she was somehow different from most other people. Indeed, she felt different, and it isolated her from others.

Her earliest ambitions were to be either a saint—she read voraciously the literature on the lives of the saints—or a healer. The two could be considered complementary, perhaps even the same in some sense, for a healer is truly a saint to the healed.

In choosing her calling, Rosemary then spent part of her life learning what all true healers must learn: they must heal themselves of their own wounds before they can heal the wounds of others. So life dealt Rosemary a series of hardships: illness and operations, a near-death experience, two failed marriages, loneliness, financial hardship, loss of friends and family, and her mother's death from cancer.

Rosemary's near-death experience happened when she was in her early twenties. She was married, with two small sons, and was working in a children's home. She was stricken with appendicitis and taken to a hospital for surgery.

"The next morning after I'd had the operation, a nurse came in and told me to sit on a chair because she had to make the bed. I wasn't feeling all that well, but I did as I was told. I felt very ill. I decided to go back and lie down on the bed again. I hoped I wouldn't get into trouble from the nurse. I just got back on the bed, and it was as if I'd passed out. I became aware of myself. I couldn't see anything. I could hear voices around me. It was as if I floated out of my body and could look down at what was going on. There was a bit of a panic, and doctors and nurses were doing something around my bedside. I thought I must be dying.

"Because my sons were very little, and there were these little children at the children's home to look after, I had a horrible thought about leaving them behind. I said prayers: 'Please don't let me die. Not for me, but for them. Just keep me alive long enough so I can bring my children up and look after this and that.

"I floated above the bed. Then I felt as though I was being drawn up a tunnel. It was the most beautiful experience. You couldn't experience anything like it on this earth. At the end of the tunnel was beauty, light, a beautiful white light, and this terrific feeling of love and paradise—something that we just don't experience here on earth. As I started to go up this tunnel, I knew I was leaving my life, and suddenly it didn't worry me. I didn't think I had to go back.

"About halfway up the tunnel, a voice said to me, 'You've got to go back now. You're not meant to come, you've got to go back.' It seemed like it was my guardian angel. I said, 'But I don't want to go back!' I felt this terrific desire to go up to paradise. But the angel said, 'No, you've got to come back, now.'

"Suddenly I was back. I woke up in the bed. I could hear the nurses talking and saying my name, but I couldn't open my eyes. And they said, 'Don't say anything about it, because ignorance is bliss.' When I came out of it, I knew something happened, but they didn't want to talk about it. The doctors and nurses kept coming up and checking me. I thought I must have stopped breathing and they resuscitated me. But it was sort of hushed up."

Rosemary said that as a result of her near-death experience, she would never be frightened of dying. "Death was an unknown before that. But now I would say to anyone, never be afraid of dying, because it is the most beautiful experience. Life is the endurance test, and when we cross over, that's when we go to heaven, and it is a very beautiful place."

One odd circumstance about Rosemary's NDE is that since childhood, she'd had a premonition that she would die young. Sometime after her brush with death, she visited a clairvoyant, who looked at her palm.

"This is very strange!" the woman said. "Your hand says you should have died by now. But you're still here!"

Rosemary confirmed her childhood premonition and her NDE. Her only conclusion was that she had a purpose yet to fulfill—perhaps a purpose that changed her original destiny.

Prior to engaging in her work as a clairvoyant, medium, and healer, Rosemary worked in hospitals as an aide. She often was aware of the presence of angels attending to the sick and dying.

On one occasion, while working at a hospital in Hawkhurst, she escorted a group of patients on an outing to the theater. During the performance, an elderly man collapsed of a heart attack. Rosemary helped him into a wheelchair and called for an ambulance. His condition deteriorated so rapidly that she had to get him out of the chair and onto the ground so that she could do mouth-to-mouth resuscitation. When the ambulance arrived, Rosemary sat in the back with him and held his hand. He was unconscious, but she had a sense that being with him and holding his hand provided him reassurance. She was also aware of angelic presences accompanying them on the trip. They were very close and closing in tighter as the ambulance traveled. She closed her eyes and concentrated on providing comfort.

The man died before the ambulance could reach the hospital. Rosemary was still clasping his hand when one of the attendants opened the ambulance door and gently took her hand away. "He's passed over now," the attendant said.

Three nights later, a presence beside Rosemary's bed awoke her from sleep. It was the elderly gentleman. Rosemary could see him plainly, as though he were still alive. He was radiating warmth and love. He had come to give her a message, which she received as a thought impression.

"Thank you," he said.

Rosemary was well into adulthood before she was ready to work with others in the type of healing work she does now. In hindsight, she realized that she had to undergo trials and traumas so that she would understand the problems of others and be able to help them.

"When I've gone through difficult times, I've asked God why this has happened to me," she said. "The answer comes back that one is never left alone, but you're not protected from all bad things. I've been pushed to the limits of my endurance, to the point where I didn't think I could stand much more. I was told I had to undergo these experiences so I would learn, in order to be able to help others. I had to learn the lesson of forgiveness, that no matter what people do, you forgive them. And I found that God is always with me.

"I asked him, what is the work I have to do? The answer came back that I had to lead people to God.

That was the work. I then began to see the reasons for my experiences, that through them I had gotten to a new level of awareness that was enabling me to grow in a spiritual way. As my awareness grew, I could see people around me being presented with lessons, and I could see whether they rejected the lessons or accepted them. And I could see how I was being used in different circumstances to help others.

"God sends suffering so that we can progress and grow spiritually. If we have a life that is easy and comfortable, at the end of it we haven't learned anything. If we have a life that has difficulties in it, then we have the chance to learn from them on the positive side.

"I've found that when people come to see me for help, almost everything they've been through, I've been through. I can immediately identify with them and say yes, I know what it's like. I've been there. That produces compassion; whereas before, I would have been sympathetic, but I wouldn't have fully understood their problems. The only way to fully understand is to actually be there yourself."

Rosemary continued, "The more difficulties you have, the more you test your faith. The more it's tested, the stronger it gets. When I look at my life, there's a loneliness. There has always been an aloneness from childhood. But the more alone you are, the more you have to turn to God for your needs. When everything is taken away, and you are in very bad difficulties, the only person you can turn to is God, and you find him within."

To develop her powers, she studied with a Spiritualist medium until he told her he could do no more for her, and she then ventured out on her own. At first, clients were a trickle of friends, and then word of mouth gained her more attention. There were articles in the press, and people from all over England began seeking her out. She then began traveling to America, where she enjoyed immediate success.

Spirit presences invariably manifest when she does a reading or healing. Some are souls of the dead, such as family members of the client. Some are guardian angels attached to the client, and some are angels who have come to assist with the healing.

The angels are accompanied by a pure, beautiful aura of silver-white light. It is a healing light, and it manifests as Rosemary places her hands on the client, and seems to flow through her hands into the person. She suddenly becomes aware of an angel—or angels—standing beside her and the client. The awareness is through the inner eye, for Rosemary works with her eyes shut.

"I do see them," Rosemary told me. "They appear not as a man or a lady, but in a sort of long white robe with fair hair. They have a white aura all around them. I find that if I tell the person that they're not alone, but that angels are always with them, it helps them a lot. Angels are something that they can identify with. I think most people want very much to feel that there is a spiritual presence close to them."

Once a woman who was fraught with anxieties over situations in her life came to see Rosemary. Rosemary gave her a reading and healing, and felt the strong silvery-white light flow through her. The woman, who was sitting with her eyes closed, said, "It's strange, but I can feel an overwhelming sense of peace."

"There's an angel right by you, that's why," responded Rosemary.

"An angel?"

"Your guardian angel," Rosemary said. Then she opened her eyes and looked at the woman. To her surprise, the woman's face was illuminated and transformed. When she had arrived for her appointment, her features had been pinched and drawn with anxiety. Now they were full and serene, and a beautiful, angelic expression graced them.

Since then, Rosemary sees facial transfigurations often during healings. "I think the whole basis of healing is to touch the soul," she said. "We're brought into this life, basically, to find God and to find ourselves in a spiritual life. When one gives healing, it's a direct link with God and angels—who are superior beings—to touch the soul of the person so that they start to grow in a spiritual way. If a person lives a materialistic life, at the end of the day, their soul passes on and they can't take their material things with them. So, if they don't develop in a spiritual way, it's a wasted life. Then they have to come back again to another life.

"If I can give a person an inner peace and also show them that they're not alone, that's one of the greatest gifts I can give. I give healing with that intent first and foremost. Then I'm helping to heal the mind, and sometimes the physical heals from that. Our Lord Jesus is the finest example of a healer. He healed spiritually, healed minds, and healed bodies, as well."

I asked Rosemary to describe some of her healings with others.

"A lady came to see me who suffered from a loss of balance, and congestion down one side of her head. I gave her healing, and she became very peaceful and serene and said she felt a lot better. Two days later she rang me up and said, 'You know, I'm feeling so much better, you put everything right.' Then her husband came to see me, and they both came back to see me. He said he was very pleased about what had been done for his wife. I thought it was the lovely angelic presence that achieved that, not me.

"Another lady had a lack of mobility in her hands and lumps on her knuckles. She was going to have an operation in the hospital. I said a little prayer to help her and gave her some healing. I was guided to work from the elbows to the wrists to the hands. Her hands were red. Afterward there were little dents on one hand where the lumps had gone down, and both hands were a nice pale color, instead of being red. The mobility came back, so that she could use the fingers."

Rosemary went on, "Another lady came to me for a reading. She said, 'I feel I am at a turning point in my life, meeting you. It has made me look at everything in a completely different way.' Readings really help some people find their pathway. People often get to a stage in life and think that there's got to be more to life than this, or which way do they turn—they're searching. The reading helped this lady onto the right pathway. I also gave her some healing for back problems she'd had for years. Later she rang me up and said that two days after having the healing, her back problems were gone, like a miracle.

"Another lady came in a state of depression and anxiety, really awful turmoil. After healing, she said she had a feeling of peace. Although we couldn't change the circumstances of the difficult marriage she was in, the healing did help her cope. She came back to see me two weeks later and told me she felt as if I'd been with her the whole two weeks. 'You didn't just pick me up and put me back on the pathway, you walked around by the side of me and held my hands,' she said. She explained that she went home from the healing, and because she felt so different, she was different with her husband, and in turn, he responded to her, and in turn, their daughter was happier. So the whole family unit became happy.

"I think everyone has a little candle inside of them," Rosemary said. "I helped to light one in her, and then she went home and lit another one in somebody else, and it spreads. It doesn't just stop at the individual healing. That person will be different, and it will either spread through their family or through their friends.

"You know, it's nice to physically heal. So you make somebody's arm better. Perhaps it just stops there. But people can cope with their physical ailments. For spiritual benefit, they must understand the reasons why they've got them, and the lessons they've got to learn as a result. Then they can basically go on and spiritually help other people. I've had a lot of people come to me who have had healing gifts handed to them, and I've been able to help them, send them out to do more good works. From one little candle, you can light a lot of lights."

Rosemary said she thought healing could be accomplished in many different ways, and that everyone has at least some ability for healing others. "I think you can heal people by talking to them, even on the phone. Sometimes by just being with them. You can write them a letter. I don't think you always have to lay hands on somebody.

"People who have come to see me and are facing difficulties in life have often said to me they could hear me talking to them in times of need, as though I were actually there with them. I think the angels take the healing to the people, wherever they are, as it's needed, even in the night while they sleep. It's one of their many missions."

═══ 10 ═══

Spirit Powers of the Native American Way

Kenneth S. Cohen, also known as Ken Bearhawk, is a renowned healer who lives in a log cabin in the mountains of Colorado. Ken is trained in various healing modalities, among them Native American and African healing and the Chinese technique of QiGong. In his work with Native American healing methods, Ken is aided by animal totems or spirit guides or helpers. Totems are roughly equivalent to the Judeo-Christian concept of angels. Their purpose is to help the spiritual development of a person and to provide sources of spiritual and psychic power. They are considered both to dwell within the body and to exist externally. Unlike the guardian angel, who comes in at birth and stays until death, totems may change during the course of a person's life, depending on spiritual development and needs.

In the Native American tradition, there are various ways that a person can find his or her path of power.

One of these is hereditary. Another is through transferral of power by an elder or medicine person. Another is through training. Ken is not Native American by birth, though he feels a profound connection to the Native American path. He has developed his healing power for more than twenty years by training and transference.

He was apprenticed to the Cherokee spiritual teacher Keetoowah Christie, the great-grandson of Ned Christie, a Cherokee hero. Keetoowah Christie transferred power into Ken's body by using a quartz crystal, which became part of his blood, his being. The use of crystal to transfer medicine power is common throughout shamanic cultures. Crystal is light made visible and represents the balance point between two worlds, the seen and the unseen, the material and the spiritual.

Ken also has been initiated into the Seneca Wolf Clan Teaching Lodge by Grandmother Twylah Nitsch (whose name means "She Whose Voice Rides On The Wind") and into the Eagle Tribe and Medicine Society by War Eagle, a Cherokee elder.

I asked Ken to describe his healing methods and to tell me about some of his experiences with totems.

"In healing, the first thing I do is counsel with the person to get a sense of their situation. That way I can determine whether I have an ability to help them. A good healer knows his strengths and limitations. There are people who come to me who I cannot help, and I make referrals. If I determine that they have a problem that I can address, especially if it is spiritual in origin, then I wait a couple of days and see if I receive guidance from my spirit helpers. Then I meet with the person again and start. I consider everything I do as complementary therapy instead of alternative therapy.

"In working with patients, first I purify them by smudging, which is using the smoke from burning sage. Some use sweet grass or cedar. I might see more about their illness through the smoke.

"I pray before, during, and after a healing, opening myself to a transpersonal source of power. I feel that when I do healing, it is not coming from me but is moving through me. I am able to connect to the Great Mystery, the Creator, who does the healing.

"I often practice noncontact healing, in which I visualize energy passing through my hands to the person. Occasionally the healing work will take the form of my placing sacred stones on their bodies. The stones have their own healing natures and are tuned through my prayer.

"There are various spiritual techniques that might be required in particular cases. For instance, I might see that a source of a person's problem is that they are out of touch with their spirit guides, their totems. If I sense that is the case, or the spirit helper has left, or the connection to the person is very tenuous, I perform a healing ceremony to reestablish contact. That can be done through prayer and calling songs that invoke the presence of a particular helper. It can also be done by waving the person's spirit helper back into the body with a feather fan or using the breath to blow the helper back into the body. Occasionally I've asked a plant, such as tobacco, which is sacred, to help me with this. I take the tobacco smoke in my mouth and blow the spirit helper back to the body with the smoke."

"How do you compare spirit helpers to angels?" I asked.

"I think they are basically the same," Ken answered. "A more interesting question is whether these helpers or angels are the same as the unconscious. I feel that the boundary between inside and outside is an imaginary one. It's a boundary of concepts, not something we actually experience. When a person is deeply in touch with himself and is practicing what Carl Jung called creative imagination, the guides that come out of the unconscious are the same as the spirit powers. On the other hand, if a person contacts the spirit powers, that is the same as reaching into the unconscious. The unconscious is not within the body —it's the other way around. The body is within the unconscious. Spirit helpers or angels are part of the collective self.

"In Native American culture, there are different ways to conceptualize the helpers, all of whom are messengers for, and aspects of, the Great Mystery. In the Seneca Wolf Clan Teaching Lodge, Grandmother Twyla speaks about four spirit band members, who are guides, who tend to appear in human form. My own visions tell me that these four band members represent the four directions, each with its own teaching. A person might not recognize or work with all of them at the same time. You might go through certain experiences in your life that help you to become aware of one particular band member, for example, the east, which is the direction of inspiration and creativity, and has the wide, panoramic vision of the eagle. After some time, you might become aware of the band members in other directions. It could take a year, it could take ten years, it could take twenty years to learn all four—it's an individual process.

"In my work, I've discovered most people have two totem animals, who are in addition to the humanlike four band members. The totems represent the conscious and the unconscious—the obvious aspect and a more hidden aspect of one's self. All—totems and band members—are sources of knowledge and wisdom. One can learn to dialogue with them, in a way analogous to the process of creative imagination. They are also actual sources of power, because they are intermediaries between the physical world and the Creator, the Great Mystery. They can be sources of power channeling. Perhaps 'funncling' is a better word. They funnel power down to us when it's needed. In shamanic cultures, if you lose touch with your power, whether it be a totem or a band member or some combination of the two, then you are vulnerable to misfortune and disease. A healing is necessary to reestablish that contact and restore power and vitality."

"How do we lose touch with our power?" I asked.

"We lose touch with our power through not following our original instructions—our assignment that the Great Mystery has written in our hearts. In other words, we lose touch by not having the courage to be fully ourselves and to follow the promptings that come from inside, and instead we're false to our medicine. For instance, we are not true to our medicine if we live our lives according to other people's expectations or the conditioning influences of educational and religious institutions. We also can be disrespectful to our medicine. For instance, if someone has a particular gift to be an artist or poet or singer, and they don't allow themselves to express that gift, they are disrespectful to their medicine, and they become sick.

"A good example is a woman I worked with one time. I felt she had a great deal of sensitivity to people and their feelings, and that this could have been turned into a real advantage in her life. She could have been a wonderful therapist. But she had so little confidence in herself because of childhood abuse that she never allowed herself to follow what she really felt should have been her authentic life-style or career. So she took up a job in business and became a manager. She didn't hate her work, but she always had an unfulfilled need to work with other people. Her sickness was chronic fatigue syndrome, which she has suffered for many years.

"When I looked at her, I saw that she had a deer and an eagle around her. Very clearly. This made sense to her—these were symbols that were relevant to her. I told her the deer was her sensitivity to energy, and the eagle was her penetrating vision or ability to look through the shells, through the masks that people use to project their social roles. She could see through that to what was authentic underneath. She began to work with those totem powers and as a result, the chronic fatigue syndrome lessened its hold on her. So, working with the spirit powers can have a very concrete effect on a person's personality and health."

"Were her totems comparable to guardian angels?"

"Yes, although totems change in the course of one's life. Sometimes new spirit powers will seek to come in to further growth and development, but a person will not make the life changes necessary to allow them in. The person will sometimes go through illness, which is due to the fact that the old spirit power has left, but the person has not made himself a fit receptable for the new spirit power that wants to come in.

"I'll give you another example of this kind of shielding. I had a student who was a street person. He panhandled for money and slept in abandoned cars in junkyards in the wintertime or slept out on the streets with drug addicts. He used to hang around classes I taught, but he never seemed to be quite 'there.' He looked like a burned-out hippie left over from the sixties. One time he came to me and said, 'I know I have problems and I want to change. What can I do?' It was the first time he had ever spoken coherently to me.

"I told him that the first step in any kind of healing is that the person has to ask to be healed. If they don't ask, nothing can be done for them. That is why healers will often ask for some kind of donation or an offering. I personally don't feel that it's right to put a monetary value on healing, but if the person doesn't give anything, then you know that they're not really asking for anything. Maybe they're just looking for a way to feel more comfortable with their problems, or they're curious, or they want entertainment or a new way to get high.

"This man really wanted to change. I asked him what he felt was his problem. He said he had no willpower. He said that whenever anyone offered him drugs or anything he could get high on, he would take them right away. 'Do you really want to stop?' I said. He said yes. I said, 'I'll tell you what you do. You cut off an inch of your hair and you burn it outside. And you say, Creator, I don't have anything. All I have is my own body. I'm offering this to you as a sign, as a release that I want something to change in my life.' I explained to him that this would be enough of an offering for me. I also said to him, 'Find someplace where you can take a bath. Go to one of the hot tubs somewhere, and get a new set of clothes. I don't care where you get them, from the Salvation Army or wherever, but put them through the laundry and get them as clean as possible. When you've taken a bath and made that offering of your hair and found new clothes, then come up to my cabin and I'll be willing to work with you.'

"He did all that, and four days later he came up to the cabin. I did a ceremony over him, smudging him and then praying over him. When I looked at him spiritually, I saw the most extraordinary thing: an eagle that was above his body. Now normally if someone is in touch with their spirit power, I can see it in their heart, but his spirit power was definitely removed and was outside of his body. On the face of the eagle there was a mask, a human face of evil intent. I used a feather to take the mask off and to discharge it. After I removed the mask, I made a prayer to the Great Mystery. I said, 'You know what is best to do with these things. We don't send them back to the ones who send them. If this mask was put on my brother here intentionally, then you know what is best to do with it.' That's the way I was taught—never send anything bad to somebody else. There are people who think that if someone can put something evil on another person, it should be sent back to them. I was taught to give it to the Creator instead.

"When I took the mask off, I could see the eagle's

natural face underneath. I shook that eagle back into my student's heart until it was resting there. When the ceremony was over, my student looked like a different person. His eyes could focus. Before that time, for all the months I had seen him in my class, his eyes could not track—they would wander all over the place. He couldn't speak more than a few words coherently, and after that could only manage broken fragments of a sentence. Now he looked like a normal human being.

"When I spoke to him about the face that I saw on the mask, it turned out that it was the exact description of someone he used to live with, some ten or more years before, in New York City. This person was apparently involved in some sort of satanic cult. My student said that it was after he left that person's home that everything went downhill in his life. He lost his job, his friends, he got divorced, he never saw his children again. He began to live off the streets. He eventually found his way to Colorado. I felt he was indeed hexed, and it was a combination of his own weakness and that other person's bad intent.

"After he had his spirit power restored, he was a different person. Within two weeks, he had a place to live, and he had gotten a job as an apprentice to a landscape gardener. He stopped taking drugs. He became very stable. In fact, he became my best student.

"To sum it up," said Ken, "The spirit powers are helpers and messengers, and they usually come to us as a grace. Our training can invite their presence, but we can't specifically stalk or track a particular power. We can only make ourselves open to it. What my elders have always told me is that the most important power, the highest power, and the one which people must always keep central in their lives—especially if they're working with the spirit powers—is the Creator, or God."

"How do we open ourselves to the spirit powers?"

"The first thing is to find out what animal you have an affinity with," Ken responded. "Some people just know that. They know that because of their dreams, or because of feelings they have when they see a certain animal—they feel like singing and dancing. If a person does not know intuitively what his totem animals are, it probably means he has not spent enough time in nature. There is no substitute for that. It's not enough to simply do guided imagery work and to imagine a situation where an animal can come to you. I feel a person must physically go out and be in nature. When you live close to nature, then these spirit animal presences, as well as the physical animals, make themselves known.

"I can give you another example of this as well. I had a client who felt victimized at work. Her boss didn't like her, and she felt her boss tried to turn other people against her. She just couldn't stand it, and she wanted to get a transfer to a different office. But that was up to her boss, who hated her, and she just felt trapped. When I asked her what animal she felt closest to, she said cats. As soon as she said it, I saw a mountain lion. I asked her how she felt about mountain lions, and she said she loved them. I knew I was on the mark.

"I said, 'All right, the mountain lion is a hunter—it is not the hunted. The mountain lion can be invisible. When you go to work this week, I want you to imagine that you are a mountain lion and that way you will not be a victim. Your boss will not notice you, or your boss will be so scared of your power that he will not say anything bad against you. Let me know what happens as a result.'

"I saw her again two weeks later. She told me she had been transferred to a different office. During the time that she was doing her visualization as a mountain lion, her boss did not notice her and did not make any rude remarks. She felt a radical difference in her health and her spirit. She was very happy with the new place and new employees she was working with."

Ken continued, "It's not only important to invite the spirit presences in, it's also important to honor them and express gratitude to them. Honoring and gratitude are the reasons for Native American songs and dances. You can go out into nature, someplace where you can be alone, and sing a song to your animal, dance it, or move like it. Some people draw a painting as a way of honoring their totems. Find some way to express gratitude, because any power or gift that you are grateful for then becomes stronger in you."

"Is prayer a good way to do that?"

"Prayer is very, very important. In the modern world, we think of prayer as asking for something. That can be part of prayer, but the most important aspect from the Native perspective is expressing gratitude—for the gift of life, for one's family, for the land, for the air, for the water, the food, for all the things that sustain us. We have to remember that there are also spiritual forces that sustain us—the Great Mystery and the various spirit helpers."

"How have you come into contact with your own spirit helpers?" I wanted to know.

"In 1977, I was passing through Colorado on my

way to California, and one day while I was taking a walk in the city there was a tremendous storm. In this area of the country, there are usually afternoon thunderstorms in the summertime, and they clear up after about an hour or two, sometimes with spectacular rainbows. This storm seemed to come from one mountain of clouds that was formed in such a perfect shape it looked like an actual mountain that was generating the lightning and thunder. This experience seemed to be a message or an omen. That night, when I went to sleep, I prayed and asked for the meaning of the vision of the storm clouds. Suddenly I sat up. I was still awake. I looked outside the window of the house to two pine trees. I saw, very clearly, two beings, one seated on each of the pine trees. On the pine tree to the left there was a red shadow. On the pine tree to the right there was a large black thunderbird. It looked almost like an eagle, but it was about nine feet long. Both of these beings communicated to me mentally. They said they were messengers that had been sent to bring me to that mountain that I saw. The next day, I should buy a pair of deerskin moccasins, take my sacred pipe, and travel west. The pipe, by the way, is a medium of prayer used in many of the Native American tribes. Natural tobacco and herbs are smoked and sent up with one's breath to the Great Mystery.

"I did as instructed the next day. I traveled through a small town, where I'm now living, and on to the top of the Continental Divide. When I got up there, at about eleven thousand or so feet, I saw the exact, real mountain that I had seen formed by the shape of the clouds the day before. There was an alpine lake. I knew that was the place I was supposed to be in. I prayed in gratitude while I was up there. This has been my special place in the world ever since.

"I went on to live in California for about four years. In 1981, I went through a difficult time emotionally and was about to start a divorce process. I knew that some physical change was needed as well and I should move and live away from the city. One evening I was doing inner work, and a woman appeared in my mind. She was a Native American, dressed in white buckskin, and was extraordinarily beautiful. She had energy pouring out of her palms. I saw that she had an amulet that looked like a huge mirror hanging around her neck. I knew I was supposed to look into that mirror. When I looked, I saw again the mountain that I had visited in 1977. I knew that I was supposed to live there, and this was a message for me to move there. Whatever I needed to be brought into my life or needed to release in terms of the pain and sorrow I was going through in the divorce, somehow all these things would come to me more easily if I was living near that mountain. So I moved within a short period of time.

"In 1984, exactly seven years from the time I had first visited that holy place, I went there on a formal vision quest. I was living in my present home, a log cabin which is about a four-hour hike to the alpine lake. I undertook the vision quest to find new meaning or direction in my life. I had gone through the divorce, I felt I was at a turning point spiritually, and the Native American spirituality was becoming much more central in the way I was living.

"As I was hiking up to the lake, something very strange happened. I experienced extreme, excruciating pain in my hip, such that I could hardly walk. I could hardly move. By the time I got to the lake, I was just dragging myself along. Storm clouds had been gathering, and once I got myself up there, thunder began to rumble. I put up my tent. The moment it was up, a terrific hailstorm started. The hailstones looked like golf balls. I was worried they were going to rip the tent apart. I was quite frightened. But I had so much pain in my body that I felt that I could not hike down from that place. Now, it was late May, very early in the season to be in such high country, and there were no other hikers or people around. I decided to take out my pipe and to ask for the meaning of this experience. And the moment I put the bowl and the stem together, the storm stopped, and a ray of light shone down on my tent. I stepped outside and there was a small eagle seated on a branch of a tree about fifteen feet away from me. The eagle took off flying to the east. I heard a voice in my mind that said, 'Now you are like the small eagle flying to the east, but soon you will be like us. Look up.' I looked up and there were two eagles circling overhead. Again I heard in my mind a voice that said, 'Always remember, there is no virtue in suffering. Only follow the way of the pipe.' It repeated itself. 'Always remember there is no virtue in suffering. Always follow the way of the pipe.' That message has stayed with me. For me, following the way of the pipe is finding a way to live that makes me as much like the pipe as possible and much like a clear channel, dedicated to the Great Mystery so the breath of the Great Mystery can move through me. It is part of my life, part of my every action. That's my dedication. My commitment.

"Seven years later, in 1991, I visited the lake again.

There were no visits in between. This is a sacred place for me and out of respect for that place, I only go when the need is there. Interestingly, this has been every seven years. In 1991, an inner voice told me I must go back to that mountain just to express gratitude that over the past seven years, I had been blessed with wonderful teachers and had been able to follow more closely my commitment.

"When I went back to the mountain, I had a feeling of total clarity up there. The first two times I had been there, in 1977 and 1984, the sky was dark and stormy. In 1991, I was going there to express gratitude for the clarity that I had felt in my life for seven years, and for the teachers and the wonderful elders that I've been blessed to work with. The sky was totally clear, and the lake water was sparkling in the most unusual way, like glittering diamonds.

"I offered my pipe to send the smoke out to the directions. Right after I finished blowing the smoke, the eagle called two times. I don't know if it was the same eagle calling twice or two eagles calling one after the other. But I knew this was an affirmation from that same power I had seen seven years earlier in my vision quest, when the two eagles had flown overhead and they had told me that I would soon be like them, just follow the way of the pipe. These eagles had stayed with me. They have given me other affirmations as well.

"Recently I went to Nevada to visit one of my dear elders and friends, Rolling Thunder, an intertribal medicine man. While I was there, I was going to offer a pipe ceremony in his honor. Just before the ceremony, a triple rainbow appeared, extending out over the desert. Beautiful! A golden eagle flew right under the arch of the rainbow. Then, a few days ago, I was up at the top of Mt. Evans here in Colorado, and got about five feet away from a mountain goat. I sat watching this mountain goat feeding for a long time, and had a wonderful feeling of communion with it. I offered the goat a little bit of tobacco in gratitude. Just as I did so, I felt something over my head, and sure enough there was an eagle circling way up overhead. So, these experiences with the eagles have been repeating themselves. You know, the elders teach us that we are not supposed to try to get the medicine. There's too much greed in the world already. In spiritual matters, we have to have the dedication, and instead of us choosing the medicine, the medicine will choose us."

"Are you aware of the eagles when you perform a healing?" I asked.

"Sometimes, yes," Ken said. "The eagle will help. Sometimes I might visualize an eagle over a person's body, fanning them. Healing depends on what kind of power is compatible with a person. I don't use a power that is incompatible with their own spirit power. I first listen to what the person has to say about their situations and try to ascertain what kind of spirit power they are working with."

Ken said that he hoped to make one more visit to his holy mountain, in 1998.

"Why do you think there will be only be one more visit?" I asked. "Your seven-year cycle could go on longer."

"My guide told me I'm supposed to visit it four times. In the Native American traditions, things happen in multiples of four or seven. Four is a number of hope—it's a quaternity, completeness in four directions. Seven is also a number of wholeness. It can imply the four directions and the three periods of time, past, present, and future, and so it embraces space and time all together. Seven is a medicine number that is revered by most Native American tribes. In fact, the number seven is so important that in some of the Cherokee ways of working with medicine, the number is said at the end of an invocation."

I asked Ken if the woman in white buckskin had appeared to him again.

"She has appeared a couple of times, but never with the same impact as that first time. I think there has not been the need on my part. I feel that the more you make your mind one with the Great Mystery and the spirits, the more you open yourself to them, and the helpers become part of your life. You don't have to use specific means to retrieve information."

Ken told me about another of his experiences involving an owl as a spirit helper. "The owl is a spirit that many Native people have a somewhat ambivalent relationship with," he said. "For instance, certain tribes will not work with the owl at all because they consider it a bringer of misfortune. Other tribes definitely feel that the owl is a helper. The owl is nocturnal. For me this association with the night gives the owl the significance of death and rebirth. I don't necessarily mean physical death and rebirth—it can be spiritual death and rebirth. In other words, dying to something that you don't need in your life anymore, making room for something that is new, that you do need.

"I had an experience with the owl when I went through a healing crisis a number of years back. I had an infection in one of my heart valves. One of my students, not knowing that I was ill, called me and asked me if I was all right. She said she'd had a frightening dream about me, in which an owl came and took my heart out of my chest, held it in his talons and took two bites out of it, and started flying to the north.

"I immediately knew that I had only four days left to live, I don't know how I knew it was four days, but somehow I just knew. My symptoms had been worsening. I had extreme pressure in the center of my chest. I couldn't walk more than a block without getting out of breath. I had pain. I was waking up in the middle of the night with severe pains in the chest. I had a generally ominous feeling about my health.

"We immediately had a ceremony in which the dreamer, the woman who called me, led it, following instructions I gave her, because she was not a Native shaman herself. She was supported by other friends, both Native and non-Native. The object of the ceremony was to invite this owl to come back from the north. Otherwise, I knew that if he got to the extreme north, I would be gone. I would cross over.

"The ceremony was successful. We asked the owl to return to spit out the pieces it had swallowed, to mend the heart, and to put it back in my chest. The owl did this. Immediately after the ceremony—and I mean immediately—all my symptoms were gone. My blood pressure, which had been way up, was down to normal, the pressure in my chest was gone. My vitality was back to normal. I was feeling fine. Earlier, an echocardiogram done at the hospital had shown I had mitral valve prolapse with some regurgitation of blood back into the atrium. The morning after the ceremony, I felt there was a structural change in my heart. I haven't had another echocardiogram done, but I have had a physician listen to my heart. There is no telltale clicking sound, unless I'm under stress."

"How did this experience influence your view of the owl?"

"I would say that the owl is a messenger of the nighttime and a messenger of transition. A being who helps one go through the dark night of the soul. The owl also can be a guide into the afterlife. It can be a symbol of death. For me, it was a potential symbol of death but became a symbol of transition."

I thanked Ken for sharing his experiences. I saw many parallels in the ways that angels work and the ways that spirit helpers work. They all come from the same source, God, or the Great Mystery.

"Working with angels or spirit powers should not be the object of one's spirituality," Ken cautioned. "These are merely helpers, and one's devotion has to be fixed on the Great Mystery, the Creator. If I meet someone who speaks too much about powers or presences, I feel they've been sidetracked, or perhaps their motivation is not right. Perhaps they're more interested in power or in the emotional thrill they get out of working with these different helpers. One's dedication really has to be centered all the time on the Great Mystery."

11

A Path of Light in Dark Times

In the opening chapters of this book, I mentioned some reasons why we are experiencing a surge in belief about angels and encounters with them. To summarize, we have a collective spiritual emptiness that cries out for more personal spiritual relationships than many of us feel we get through conventional religious channels. Angels are part of our mythology, and we are attempting to reclaim the riches of our mythological tradition, which have been buried by science and technology. Also, we are in need of great help because we have great problems, on both individual and global scales. And interest in angels follows a more general trend over the past fifty years or so of increased openness to the paranormal and an increased willingness to discuss paranormal experiences.

One important reason we are having more angel experiences is a collective uplifting and expansion of human consciousness to higher levels, which provides us greater access to nonordinary realities.

I subscribe to the view that we are multidimensional beings. Throughout history we have developed worldviews—and the scientific paradigm—that in essence have encased us in a three-dimensional reality. I believe that our consciousness does have access to other realities we call nonordinary. Angels dwell in a "nonordinary" reality, as do other beings from our mythologies, such as fairies and nature spirits. Because these nonordinary realities are very different from our three-dimensional world, they have fantastical or dreamlike qualities to them, but they are just as real as the physical world we inhabit. We are able to experience these other realities when openings occur. Openings may be caused by a synchronistic coming together of right time, right place, right state of mind.

These breakthroughs to other realities seem to be on the increase in modern times. The increase is due to three factors: 1) the overall increase in world population, hence more anecdotes; 2) an increased willingness to disclose exceptional experiences; and 3) an evolutionary advance in our collective consciousness that is pulling us into other realities, which is the expression of the true nature of our unlimited, multidimensional consciousness.

Thus, we are, at least in the West, seeing an increasing percentage of the adult population acknowledging exceptional experiences. For example, in 1889, the Society for Psychical Research in London conducted a

Census of Hallucinations to gather statistics on apparitions. This census, plus similar studies carried out in the United States, France, and Germany showed that about 10 percent of the adult population reported an experience involving an apparition. Today, roughly half the adult population in the United States alone reports some type of apparitional experience. As I have said, some of that increase can be accounted for by a greater willingness to admit such experiences.

Nonetheless, paranormal phenomena themselves seem to be on the rise: apparitions, UFO encounters, visions of the Blessed Virgin Mary, encounters with angels, out-of-body experiences (which may or may not be paranormal), near-death experiences, and psychic experiences in general (clairvoyance, telepathy, precognition, psychokinesis, etc.). All these things take us into nonordinary realities. These openings are being presented to us as preparation for an uplifting of human consciousness to higher and more subtle levels.

The upward rising of human consciousness is not a new idea, though opinions have varied as to the speed and process of expansion. Teilhard de Chardin, for example, was influenced by Henri-Louis Bergson's *Creative Evolution,* which argued against dualism in favor of an evolving universe. Teilhard conceived of a cosmic evolution in four phases: galactic, earth, life, and human, all of which depend on the integration of the psychic with the physical. Evolution implies the law of "complexification," which means that as physical matter becomes more complex, so does consciousness, which is intrinsic to all life-forms. Thus the human race has arisen from, and is connected to, all other life-forms on earth, both physically and psychically. In its human form, evolution becomes conscious of itself. The convergence of various human groups progressively will shape the ultrahuman, a process now under way. The ultimate goal is a convergence toward Christ, the "Omega point" at which human consciousness finds the ultimate integrity and unity.

Teilhard used such words as *cosmogenesis,* for the development of a world with man at its center; *noosphere,* a collective human consciousness within the biosphere of the earth; *noogenesis,* for the growth of humankind's mind; *hominization* and *ultrahominization,* for the future stages of man's transcendent humanization. The increasing numbers of humans and the improving communication are fusing all parts of the noosphere together, Teilhard said. As a result, humankind will achieve more integrated and intense mental activity, which will facilitate the upward climb to higher stages of hominization.

Teilhard believed that the evolution of human consciousness would take place over millions of years. Others, however, see changes occurring at a much faster rate.

Gerald S. Hawkins, the British-American astronomer and mathematician famous for demonstrating that Stonehenge was an ancient observatory (*Stonehenge Decoded* and *Beyond Stonehenge*), has conceived of "mindsteps," or stages in the upward progress of the collective human mind. In his book *Mindsteps to the Cosmos* (1983), Hawkins likens mindsteps to a staircase, each step of which takes the collective mind further along in its understanding of the relationship of humans to the cosmos. Mindsteps are not the same as paradigms or new worldviews, Hawkins says. Rather, they are examples of both, but are more dramatic and are irreversible.

Mindsteps are also cumulative, building one on the other with some overlap. The changes in collective thinking wrought at each step depend on the accumulated growth at the previous level. For example, Copernicus's heliocentric discovery actually was put forward in 270 B.C. by Aristarchus—but the human collective simply wasn't ready for it, and Aristarchus was denounced for impiety by the Stoics. Even by Copernicus's time, heliocentrism still came as a tremendous shock.

Hawkins proposes five mindsteps, from 35,000 B.C. to the present time. Each successive step is shorter in duration, suggesting that we are heading through ever-faster changes in collective consciousness.

Mindstep 0, beginning in 35,000 B.C. and lasting for 32,000 years, was the Age of Chaos, in which the cosmos was seen, registered in the human mind, but left unexplained. Mindstep 1, beginning in 3,000 B.C. and lasting 3,150 years, ushered in the Age of Myth and Legend, in which the sun, moon, stars, and planets were explained by stories. It ended with the work of astronomer-mathematician Ptolemy.

Mindstep 2, beginning in A.D. 150 and lasting 1,393 years, was the Age of Order, which Copernicus brought to an end. Mindstep 3, beginning in 1543 and lasting 383 years, brought the Age of Revolution, and the discoveries of science. Mindstep 4, beginning in 1926, heralded the Age of Space, our present mindstep.

By doing some calculations, Hawkins estimated that Mindstep 5 would arrive around 2021, followed by Mindsteps 6 and 7 in 2045 and 2051, respectively. Mindstep 5 might feature contact with extra-terrestrials. Mindstep 6 might usher in an omega era called the Age of Spirit, which might see the development of time travel. Writes Hawkins, "Mindstep 6 could be proof of, the demonstration of the existence of, something unseen, a new type of field connected with life, the existence of which is so persuasive that its general acceptance is inevitable. In religious contexts it could be identified with the world of the spirit. In this area there are scientific indicators which may or may not be precursors. There are the broad questions of telepathy, existence or not of a vital force, the existence of the soul, and continuation of life after death. Then there are the unmeasurable human emotions of love, friendship, hate, pleasure, and pain. Are these all interlocking parts of a nonphysical cosmos?"

Hawkins's mindstep ideas were published ten years ago. I believe that we've moved along much faster, and that we are already in Mindstep 5, heading into Mindstep 6. We haven't had proof positive of extraterrestrial contact, as Hawkins mentioned might occur in Mindstep 5, although some would argue that contact has long been established. We are, however, pushing the edges of our collective consciousness into the nonphysical cosmos. We are more than shifting a paradigm—we are engaged in a consciousness revolution.

I believe that angels are manifesting more dramatically, and in greater numbers, to help us in this transformation of consciousness. For when we open up, we are vulnerable not only to the agents of light but to the agents of darkness as well.

Angels of Darkness

So far I haven't talked much about the dark angels —those who fell with Lucifer to become the demons who try to lead us astray, away from the light of God. Dark angels do exist. Just like the angels of light, they are among us. And, just like the angels of light, they can assume many forms and approach us in many ways. They may be the ugly demons described in medieval writings, but more often than not, they approach us in the guise of humans so that we let down our guard. Like angels of light, they can appear as mysterious strangers. They can come at us through other people—individuals whom we trust but whose various weaknesses allow the penetration of darkness into their beings and who may act unwittingly in carrying out the intent of the dark forces.

The purpose of the dark angels is at the least to neutralize us as centers of light and love and, if necessary, to destroy us—spiritually, psychically, even physically. They are engaged in spiritual warfare with the forces of light for control of our souls. The more we can be encouraged to petty acts of meanness and falsehood, to major acts of destruction and violence—the more we empty our souls of light and fill them instead with darkness—the stronger the dark angels become, and the further away we fall from God. The choice is ours, because both the forces of light and the forces of darkness present themselves to us. We choose which ones we want to follow. And when we choose darkness, the angels of light cannot rescue us unless we realize the folly of our choice and turn to them for help. When we ask, even with the smallest cry of despair, the smallest prayer, the help is given in the greatest abundance and love.

The struggle for our souls has picked up speed as we go deeper into the expansion of consciousness. The openings of our consciousness to other realities holds the promise to bring us closer to God. As a result, the angels of darkness have intensified their efforts to push us off the path. As we open up, we can become more vulnerable, too, if we are not careful, for the dark forces have more avenues to use in their work against us.

I do not wish to be an alarmist. By no means. For if we start mistrusting the agents of light, fearing that they are demons in disguise, then we paralyze ourselves—which is precisely what the dark side wants. They would like us to trust nothing and encase ourselves trembling in fear. Fear is the best weapon the darkness has. Fear is the fertile breeding ground for all evil—for hatred, anger, jealousy, greed, lusts and addictions of all kinds. Fear kills. It kills the spirit. When acted out in violence, it kills the body, the vehicle through which the soul can experience spiritual growth.

The engines of darkness have terrible power, but nonetheless, they cannot stand up to the greater, more awesome power of light and love. Light dissolves the dark.

The angels of light and dark watch each soul. The dark ones have a harder time getting recruits, for there are not many who consciously dedicate themselves to the path of darkness and evil. Rather, some people fall onto that path through temptation, and thus they are recruited indirectly. Most people want to lead righteous, good lives, and so they pledge themselves to the path of light.

Either way, when choices are made, the forces of light and dark are set in motion, pulling and pushing, struggling for dominance. Calls go out into the spirit world. For every soul who treads the path of light, the angels of darkness assess what it will take to knock him or her off. The greater the soul's own light, and the more influential that soul is in bringing others to the light, the harder the dark forces work to destroy. In a serious battle, the soul may be sucked into a downward spiral. The mundane life may unravel. There may be illness, misfortune, and personal and professional difficulties. Inevitably, there will be severe tests of character. If the tests are passed, the hold of the dark forces is broken, and they will not be able to attack the soul in such a manner again. The angels of light pour in and increase the shielding around the soul. Furthermore, the soul is lifted to a new level of even greater light and effectiveness. To win a fight with the dark angels is empowering.

As the spiritual warfare escalates, we must constantly reaffirm our commitment to the path of light. We must dedicate our souls to unconditional love. We must ask God's agents, the angels of light, to protect us and guide us, and keep us to the straight path. We must banish the dark angels.

In my sessions with Eddie Burks, I asked him what he thought about dark angels.

"I think that just as we have dark spirits among us, we have souls that fall away into dark regions when they die, not permanently, but sometimes for a long time," answered Eddie. "Then there are corresponding angelic beings who are operating at that dark level. I believe in the existence of the archangel Michael and of the fallen angel Lucifer: I once had a most extraordinary encounter with the dark angel Lucifer, or a representative of his. I saw a figure and he had a black cloak on. His face was extraordinarily handsome, and he had curly hair. No horns, I hasten to add. His face was dark, not like a black man's face, but it was dark and it shone—it was reflecting light. And as I watched him, he opened its cloak so that one could see the lining within the cloak, and the lining shone a brilliant silver light. I was told that Lucifer longs to show his other self."

Eddie's encounter with Lucifer came in 1987 during a reading. Three messages by an entity called Jester were given before Eddie was shown the true identity of the being behind them.

The first message was this:

"'All this will pass,' meaning all the frenetic activity we are aware of. It will be locked up as though it were a bad dream, the dream that humanity had to have. At the present time there are many treading the earth path, for this will be perhaps their last opportunity on this planet. This is the harshest planet but also the one that offers the fastest learning. Do not be dismayed by this, for it is all part of the great plan. The things of which you have spoken [the affinity of the natural world of the North American Indian] will come again for there will be peace that will allow this. However, it will never be the same as it was on the great plains of America. It will be more consciously directed and will be on a universal scale, but first there has to be much clearing away, much cleaning up. It is important that the earth cleansing is first carried out at the astral level, for this is where these things must always start. Cleaning up at the earth level will then take place more easily and more naturally. You will understand this better if you think of the earth as an organism, which in reality it is. Apply then the holistic approach to earth itself."

The second message dealt with earth changes:

"As the sands change and level under the incoming waves of the rising tide, so will earthly things change. You must be ready for these changes.

"Anticipate nothing but be prepared for anything. A spiritual poise and the ability to see past the events; these things will become important. Fear will be the worst enemy.

"This is not immediate, but those with awareness will be able to read the signs before the events. It will be well orchestrated. The birth pangs of a new age.

"All we need do is keep on learning, preparing, increasing our awareness, increasing the web of love and service. Those who walk in the light will have no fear.

"The slumbering earth will awaken to her new role. She will be cleansed. 'And there was a new earth and a new heaven.'

"See the majesty of God's purpose in all this. This message is meant only for those who understand, who walk in the light."

The tone of Jester's third message was "an unaccustomed seriousness," according to Eddie:

"Do not be cast down by what you have been told. Listen carefully and behind it all you will become aware of the choirs of heaven, of great rejoicing that it will come about so, for it could be otherwise. It could have become truly cataclysmal, and had that been so, it would have called for a new beginning. This way, there will be a measured continuity. Praise be to God, and don't be dismayed to realize that you are playing your part in these necessary changes."

As this message was being given, Eddie saw the sign of the cross being traced. The messages had to be taken as a whole, he realized, in order to achieve a balanced understanding of them. "You will see the importance of the order in which they have been brought," he was told.

Eddie then was shown the true identity of Jester, and recorded his impression:

"I have an impression of the being responsible for generating these three messages. A strange impression, not an ordinary spirit at all. It's a little bit like an angelic being, but not an ordinary angelic being. He has a cloak, and his aspect is dark, but not evil.

"When he opens his cloak and shows us the inside texture, it is of a brilliant metallic silver. I see it as white, slightly blue, and as silver. I am tempted to think it is one of the servants of Lucifer, who shows darkness on the outside. His face is dark. He opens his cloak and shows on the inside this brilliant white, and he has been waiting to reverse his cloak. He is a being of great power, but not of the angelic host. Neither is he an evolved human spirit. He is closely linked with the archangel Michael in apparent opposition."

Eddie was then told by the being, "It would not be good for you to be shown any more."

"Why do you think Lucifer revealed himself to you?" I asked.

"The meaning that came through to me was that Lucifer was really doing God's work, however devious that may seem, and that he longed for the time when, having done this work, he could resume his former role amongst the white angels.

"I think that what he does is to bring the idea and the reality of evil into the world to give us an alternative path to follow. In offering us this choice between good and evil, he is making it possible for us to gain experience of the dark side and to gain experience in depth in more than one sense. We gradually learn, over many lifetimes, to climb out of that dark pit that we dig for ourselves. Having climbed out of it, we've learned a great deal, we've become much wiser. We have a wisdom that couldn't come about simply from purity.

"I think Lucifer's function is to be continuously offering us what the Bible refers to as temptation, but I tend to think of it as the alternative power," Eddie went on. "At every stage in our lives, we're offered this other path. Without this notion of evil, without his presence, we humans would be much more like the angelic kingdom. It is through Lucifer's intervention that we get ourselves in a mess and that we learn through our own suffering."

There are different ways to interpret Eddie's experiences with the Lucifer energy. A conservative, fundamentalist approach would say that Lucifer's light is just another one of his tricks to deceive us into thinking he might not be so bad after all. On the other hand, perhaps Lucifer truly seeks to be redeemed himself. If human souls who fall into darkness can be redeemed, cannot dark angels as well? Is redemption to be denied them forever? If we are to pull ourselves up into God's light, then perhaps we pull up the angels of darkness along with us—we transmute them as well as ourselves. As long as there is darkness in the human soul, the fallen angels cannot be redeemed.

Evaluating Angel Encounters

An encounter with an angel does not truly benefit us unless we have a way of interpreting it so that it makes sense to us in terms of our worldview, and we can integrate it—that is, accept it as a real experience. If we are ambivalent about angels and one manifests to us to rescue us from disaster, we gain nothing beyond the luck of the rescue if it does not alter our beliefs about angels and in turn our beliefs about ourselves, our souls, and our relationship to God.

Encounters with angels are part of a broader spectrum of unusual experiences that incorporate altered states of consciousness, nonordinary realities, psychic phenomena, and elements of the mystical. Various terms have been given to these experiences. "Extraordinary experience" is one, favored by Kenneth S. Ring, a leading researcher in near-death experiences. "Transcendent experience" and "transpersonal experience" are others. Psychologist Abraham H. Maslow, who pioneered humanistic and transpersonal psychologies, coined the term "peak experience" to describe nonreligious, quasi-mystical episodes as sudden flashes of intense happiness and well-being, and awareness of the "ultimate truth" and unity of all things. Such peak experiences can be part of angel experiences.

Parapsychologist Rhea A. White coined the term "exceptional human experience" as a generic term for an entire class of experiences that are discrete and unrelated. White recognizes that such experiences have an individual element—that is, it is up to the experiencer to determine whether or not the experience is "exceptional."

For guidance on how to evaluate our experiences with angels, we cannot necessarily turn to religion. As was pointed out in chapter 1, modern religion has been rather uncomfortable with the question of angels. We can find no unilateral support for them.

Nor can we turn to science. In the secular world, exceptional human experiences have been treated with a jaundiced eye. They do not fit into the scientific paradigm. They cannot be measured, quantified, or qualified. They cannot be replicated in controlled experiments, and they cannot be fit into a table of statistics. Science tends at best to disregard them, if not deny them altogether. The field of parapsychology, which has attempted a scientific examination of psychic phenomena, has struggled along for more than a century hamstrung by the scientific paradigm. Extrasensory perception, psychokinesis (mind over matter), out-of-body experience, and such are square pegs that won't fit into the round holes of scientific protocol.

When psychical research became organized with a scientific bent in the late nineteenth century, first in England and most notably under the banner of the Society for Psychical Research, one of the first questions addressed was, Is there survival after death? Researchers investigated numerous mediums who claimed to communicate with the dead, looking for proof that what they received did in fact come from the Other Side. They collected numerous anecdotal accounts of apparitions. They attempted to record the presence of apparitions using scientific equipment. They accumulated piles of evidence in support of survival but no proof that the scientific world could accept. "Evidence in support of" is, in science, light-years away from proof. Only a few decades ago, parapsychologists generally abandoned trying to prove survival. They had not been able to discover even the limits of psi (extrasensory perception and psychokinesis) in the living, let alone how to differentiate psi coming from the dead. The result is that science still officially denies survival, and even many parapsychologists—who are supposed to push out the psychic frontiers—are at the very least skeptical about it. Thus, if science denies survival after death, how can it contend with the existence of angels, who are inextricably bound up in the fates of our souls?

The answer is that science cannot give us much help in dealing with exceptional experiences, which are subjective.

Therefore, we are left to our own devices—our own worldviews, our own cultural beliefs, our own religious beliefs—when it comes to accepting and interpreting the existence and activities of angels, as well as any other exceptional experience that might happen to us.

At the 1992 annual conference of the Academy of Religion and Psychical Research held in Rosemont, Pennsylvania, Rhea White took parapsychology to task for its shortsightedness in ignoring exceptional human experience. Such experiences can alter lives. More often than not, they open us up to additional exceptional experiences. "I think the lesson EHEs [exceptional human experiences] can teach is more than simply that limits may be transcended and that our nature and that of reality may be potentially limitless," she said. "I think that in studying EHEs we may be stepping right inside the workshop where 'reality' is being re-created at every moment."

An exception to this shortsightedness is the groundbreaking research that has been done in near-death experiences. Were NDE researchers to follow strict scientific protocols, they would first have to prove that people really died and came back, for near death is not death. When you really die, you don't come back, and therefore cannot report your encounters with tunnels and angels and other beings of light. NDE researchers have acknowledged that it is unlikely, if not impossible, to prove that what happens in near death is the same as what happens in death. Instead, they have looked beyond to learn more about the nature of NDEs and *how these experiences transform people.*

Transformation. That is the matter central to all exceptional experiences. If we cannot prove empirically that they happen, must it end there? *Something* happens, and a person is altered, sometimes for life. We must focus instead on accepting our experiences and coming to terms with how they change us. I can only echo White when she said that exceptional human experiences are seeds of transcendence—they are calls to change, growth, and transcendence of the boundaries one has set in life. "If dreams are the royal road to the unconscious, then possibly EHEs are the royal road to heightened consciousness—possibly even to eventual enlightenment," she said. Angels are part of that grand picture.

So how do we validate and integrate our experiences with angels? Angels give us something positive and useful, whether it is information, inspiration, or reaffirmation of self-worth. They bring positive, not negative, experiences that open up doorways to life, or doorways to other realities—or both. They connect us to the highest and deepest parts of ourselves, to each other, to all things, and to God.

Believing in angels, or thinking about angels, especially if one has had angel encounters, encourages more experiences of the same sort. Philosopher Michael Grosso calls this the "mirror factor of the psychic universe." The psychic universe reflects back to us what we believe, and we then experience what we believe. The stronger our beliefs, the more feedback we get in terms of experiences.

There do seem to be limits for many of us, however. Witness some of the people who spoke in the pages of this book, describing an experience that remains indelible throughout life. They wish for another like it, but none comes.

I believe that angels resort to drama only when necessary, in order to break through our barriers of consciousness. Once they have broken through, they can commune with us on more subtle planes. All of the persons who'd had dramatic experiences did feel continually in the guiding presence of angels thereafter.

We may wish for drama—don't we all love good entertainment?—but drama is not required in order to meet with angels. In fact, the angels would prefer not to use a heavy hand. They would rather not crash about in the material world. They would much rather have us attune ourselves to the frequencies of a higher consciousness, to the true music of our souls. When we do that, and we listen carefully, we can hear the angels singing. They give us their songs of guidance. They sing God's love.

Everyone possesses the gifts necessary for communing with angels, whether it be through visionary experience, clairaudience, or the intuitive voice. "You have to want the communion, and make the commitment to the angels to work with them," said Jane M. Howard. "Most of all, you have to be responsible. What are you going to do with the results? If you're sincere about growing and helping other people, the angels will be glad to work with you. Expect miracles."

One can invest too much in angels, however. We can turn them into idols, which would upset the balance of our relationship with them. We can also trivialize angels with pop-culture cuteness. Angels are not dolls or pets, or doilies for tea parties. They are awesome beings deserving of great respect. As the angels told me in that session with Eddie Burks: *Do not reduce us in any way to suit humanity's understanding. This would not be right. Raise humanity instead to meet us through inspired understanding. Impress on people that we are not as they. We are not human. We are no closer to God than you are. But we serve his purpose in a way that you would judge to be more direct.*

A number of persons interviewed for this book supported the belief that angels cannot help us unless we invite them to do so. In some cases, the individuals themselves were told that by angels. Or it was not until they faced a crisis that they asked for help.

We can ask for help in many ways. Sometimes we ask for help unconsciously, that is, through our higher selves. We can facilitate the interaction with angels by direct invitation, especially through prayer, meditation, and visualization. And while we can ask for ourselves, we will achieve far more if we ask for help for others—our angels working through the angels that protect other people, like some of the popes have done, as described in chapter 1.

Always give thanks first. Give thanks for the blessings in life and the opportunities that lie ahead. Give thanks for the guidance that is being sought. It will be given.

Remember the words of the angels: *We bear the very essence of unconditional love.*

Resources

The following organizations and individuals may be contacted. When writing for information and prices of goods and services, please *enclose a self-addressed stamped envelope.*

Jane M. Howard
Angel Heights
P.O. Box 95
Upperco, MD 21155
410-833-9612

Angel readings, lectures, workshops.

Eileen Eilas Freeman
AngelWatch Network and *The AngelWatch Journal*
P.O. Box 1362
Mountainside, NJ 07092

Newsletter, information clearinghouse.

RESOURCES

Alma Daniel
c/o Eldorado
300 Central Park West
New York, NY 10024

Meditations, classes, lectures, and workshops in spiritual development.

Kenneth S. Cohen
P.O. Box 234
Nederland, CO 80466

Lectures, workshops in healing; healing work.

Rosemary Gardner Loveday
Poppy Cottage
2 Chapel Row
Huthfield Near Ashford
Kent TN25 4LP, England

Readings and healings in the U.K. and U.S.

Roseann Cervelli
2221 April Drive
Martinsville, NJ 08836

Angel channeling.

Bibliography and Suggested Reading

Burnham, Sophy. *A Book of Angels*. New York: Ballantine Books, 1990.

————. *Angel Letters*. New York: Ballantine Books, 1991.

Cervelli, Roseann. *Voices of Love*. Farmingdale, NY: Coleman Publishing, 1986.

Daniel, Alma, Timothy Wyllie, and Andrew Ramer. *Ask Your Angels*. New York: Ballantine Books, 1992.

Davidson, Gustav. *A Dictionary of Angels*. New York: The Free Press, 1967.

Evans, Hilary. *Visions*Apparitions*Alien Visitors*. Wellingborough, England: Aquarian Press, 1984.

————. *Gods*Spirits*Cosmic Guardians*. Wellingborough, England: Aquarian Press, 1987.

————. *Alternate States of Consciousness*. Wellingborough, England: Aquarian Press, 1989.

Freeman, Eileen Eilas. *Touched by Angels*. New York: Warner Books, 1993.

Godwin, Malcolm. *Angels: An Endangered Species*. New York: Simon & Schuster, 1990.

Graham, Billy. *Angels: God's Secret Agents*. New York: Doubleday, 1975.

Grant, Jack. *Companions in Spirit*. Berkeley, Calif.: Celestial Arts, 1984.

Hodson, Geoffrey. *The Brotherhood of Angels and Men*. Wheaton, Ill: Quest Books, 1982. First published 1927.

Howard, Jane M. *Commune with the Angels*. Virginia Beach, Va.: A.R.E. Press, 1992.

Huber, Georges. *My Angel Will Go Before You*. Westminster, Md.: Four Courts Press, 1983.

Humann, Harvey. *The Many Faces of Angels*. Marina del Rey, Calif.: Devorss Publications, 1986.

Laurence, Richard, trans. *The Book of Enoch the Prophet*. San Diego: Wizards Bookshelf, 1983.

McLean, Adam, ed. *A Treatise on Angel Magic*. Grand Rapids, Mich.: Phanes Press, 1990.

Maclean, Dorothy. *To Hear the Angels Sing*. Hudson, N.Y.: Lindisfarne Press, 1980.

MacGregor, Geddes. *Angels: Ministers of Grace*. New York: Paragon House, 1988.

Mallasz, Gitta, transcribed. *Talking with Angels*. Einseideln, Germany: Daimon Verlag, 1988.

Moolenburgh, H. C. *A Handbook of Angels*. Walden, England: C. W. Daniel, 1984.

————. *Meetings with Angels*. Walden, England: C. W. Daniel, 1991.

Parente, Fr. Allesio. *Send Me Your Guardian Angel, Padre Pio*. Foggia, Italy: Editions, 1961.

Parisen, Maria, comp. *Angels and Mortals: Their Co-Creative Power*. Wheaton, Ill: Quest Books, 1990.

Pseudo-Dionysius: The Complete Works. New York: Paulist Press, 1987.

Ronner, John. *Do You Have a Guardian Angel?* Murfreesboro, Tenn.: Mamre Press, 1985.

BIBLIOGRAPHY AND SUGGESTED READING

Snell, Joy. *The Ministry of Angels*. New York: The Citadel Press, 1959.

Taylor, Terry Lynn. *Messenger of Light: The Angels' Guide to Spiritual Growth*. Tiburon, Calif.: H. J. Kramer, 1990.

——————. *Guardians of Hope: The Angels' Guide to Personal Growth*. Tiburon, Calif.: H. J. Kramer, 1992.

——————. *Answers from the Angels: A Book of Angel Letters*. Tiburon, Calif.: H. J. Kramer, 1993.

Wyllie, Timothy. *Dolphins*Extraterrestrials*Angels*. Ft. Wayne, Ind.: Bozon Enterprises, 1984.

Explore the Powers of the Mind and Beyond

DEVELOP YOUR PSYCHIC ABILITIES
by Litany Burns 70138-X/$5.99

POWER ASTROLOGY
by Robert McNaughton 67181-2/$5.50

FULL CIRCLE:
The Near Death Experience And Beyond
by Barbara Harris and Lionel C. Bascom;
Commentary by Bruce Greyson, M.D.
68616-X/$5.99

ANGELS OF MERCY
by Rosemary Ellen Guiley 77094-2/$5.50

Available from Pocket Books

POCKET BOOKS